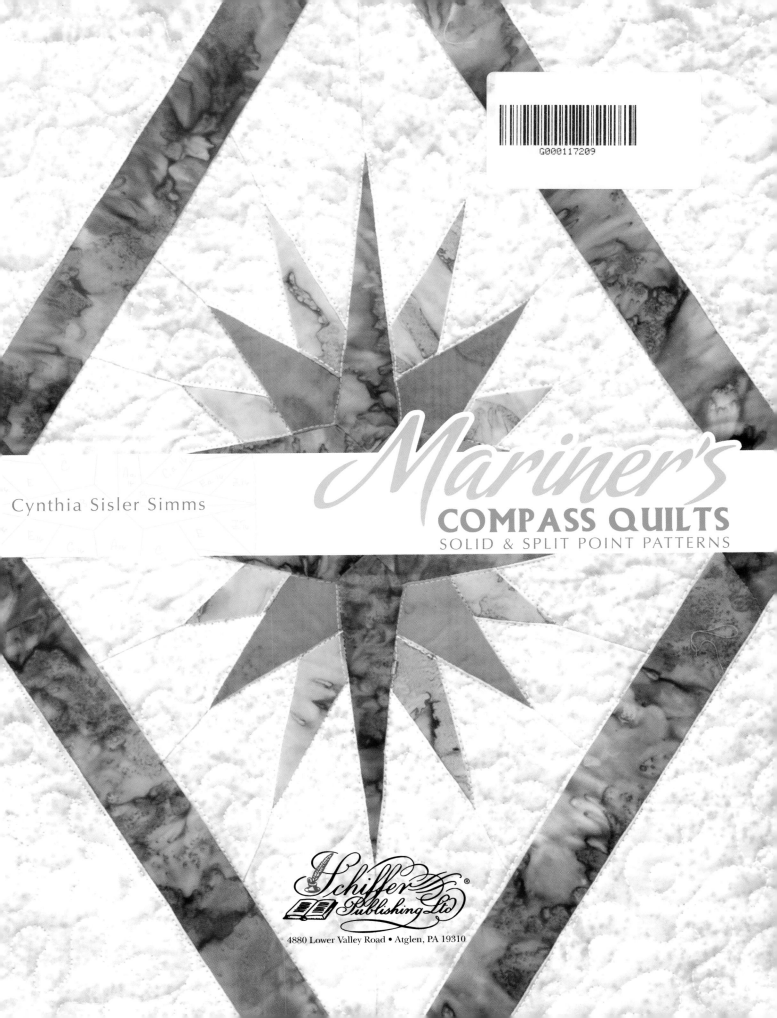

Cynthia Sisler Simms

Mariner's
COMPASS QUILTS
SOLID & SPLIT POINT PATTERNS

Schiffer *Publishing Ltd*®

4880 Lower Valley Road • Atglen, PA 19310

Other Schiffer Books on Related Subjects:
Creating Celebration Quilts. Cyndi Souder. ISBN: 978-0-7643-4350-6. $19.99
Creating Children's Artwork Quilts. Shannon Gingrich Shirley. ISBN: 978-0-7643-4180-9. $16.99
Cutting-Edge Art Quilts. Mary W. Kerr. ISBN: 978-0-7643-4313-1. $34.99
New Quilts: Interpretations & Innovations. Nancy Rae. ISBN: 978-0-8874-0157-2. $14.95

Designed by Justin Watkinson
Type set in Amorinda/Optima LT Std/Aldine 721 BT

ISBN: 978-0-7643-4525-8
Printed in the United States

Published by Schiffer Publishing, Ltd.
4880 Lower Valley Road
Atglen, PA 19310
Phone: (610) 593-1777; Fax: (610) 593-2002
E-mail: Info@schifferbooks.com

For the largest selection of fine reference books on this and related subjects, please visit our website at **www.schifferbooks.com**. You may also write for a free catalog.

This book may be purchased from the publisher.
Please try your bookstore first.

We are always looking for people to write books on new and related subjects.
If you have an idea for a book, please contact us at
proposals@schifferbooks.com

Schiffer Books are available at special discounts for bulk purchases for sales promotions or premiums. Special editions, including personalized covers, corporate imprints, and excerpts can be created in large quantities for special needs. For more information contact the publisher.

Contents

Dedication

To my Grandmothers—for the scraps, patterns, and time; also, for instilling an appreciation of skills, workmanship, and beauty of quilts.

To my Mother—for all the sewing skills she taught me.

To my Husband and Daughters—Ray, for knowing the importance of quilting and encouraging me. The girls for knowing I put all my love for them into a quilt for each of them.

To my Friends and Students—whose friendship, enthusiasm, and ideas for quilting kept me on my toes, expanding my imagination and, hopefully, theirs.

—Cynthia Sisler Simms

Life

My life is a crazy quilt
But there's no use to fret.
God will put it together
And make my life a pattern yet.

Patch upon patch, making my life
Yellow for friendship,
Red for love,
Calico for endurance, gingham for faith,
White for purity sent from God above.

My life is a crazy quilt,
But there's no use to fret.
God will put it all together
And make my life a pattern yet.

Calico for a mother so dear,
Who guided my every step;
Checks for a father strong,
Who cuddled me on his lap.

Prints of many colors,
The many loving friends;
Ginghams are for my children,
On whom my life depends.

My life is a crazy quilt
That has been put in order.
God filled it with happiness;
Love circles it for a border.
My life is a pattern now.

—Mabel Lewis Sisler

Introduction

The main purpose of this book is to introduce new patterns and shapes for a traditional pattern, the Mariner's Compass. Most compass patterns today are round shaped. Here, I have created new patterns beginning with an oval shape, eliminating the curved edge, and replaced it with a choice of block shapes: hexagon, rectangle, and diamond. Each compass can be done in all three block shapes. I combined these ideas with a semi-miniature style to create semi-miniature Mariner's Compasses. There are eight different patterns, each in two sizes, one 5" x 8" and the other 6" x 10", which totals sixteen patterns. On each compass, there are three different variations from which to choose: Solid Points, Split Points, or a combination of Solid and Split Points.

If you are proficient with machine piecing, you should be able to construct these by machine—including the curved seam if used—with the exception of the centers. They should be set in by hand to ensure a smooth fit. Also, instead of piecing the center piece, you also have the option of appliqueing it on.

As a quilter and an Army wife, the Mariner's Compass not only fascinated me, but also has special meaning. As a quilter, I learned early that the round Mariner's Compass is a traditional pattern. As a military wife of twenty years, I was sent all over the world with my husband. The Mariner's Compass, to me, points to the way home.

Being a quilter for close to forty years, a quilting teacher for over eighteen years, and attending quilt shows, workshops, and even in my classes, the sayings most often heard when viewing a Mariner's Compass are: "That's too hard for me to do," "It's an advanced quilt pattern," or "It has curved piecing in it." I say, emphatically, "Wrong!" to the first two and have changed the third. This pattern is often considered advanced because of the many points and construction. However, it is as easy to put together as any other pattern. Each pattern has a sequence in which the pieces are put together. You either start each square side to side, top to bottom, or from the center out, depending upon the pattern. With the compass, whether round or oval, you start from the outside and work to the center. There are a good many round compasses available, but few compare to the amount of other traditional patterns.

Most compasses in quilting are done in a circle with 8 to 16 to 32 to 64 points, depending upon the pattern being used. They also range from a 12-inch to 30-inch square or larger, depending upon the individual taste.

Several compasses have been elongated into an oval to form a large rectangle used in centers of quilts for a medallion effect.

Novice quilters are under the impression that a Mariner's Compass is a pattern for advanced quilters. In my classes, I have all four levels of quilters, and all have enjoyed doing a Mariner's Compass. All have stated later that it was not as difficult to put together as it appeared. Some have stated that they are glad they know how to put one together but would not want to do another.

The compass was used to indicate direction of North, East, South, West, and points in between.

Miniatures are coming into their own now and are used as wall hangings and in miniature doll houses.

On the following pages, you will find a collection of oval Mariner's Compasses. The miniatures go up to only 16 points so that the pattern pieces are still easy to work with. Also included are directions on drafting ovals and Mariner's Compasses, so that you may draft a pattern to whatever size you would like. Instructions are the same for both hand and machine piecing, with the exception of certain centers.

One fourth of each compass pattern shows that you can do a split point or use a stripe-print fabric to get the same effect. You can do all solid prints, all split points, or a combination of the two. The choice is yours. Usually when piecing, I sew down my seams so that they all lay flat. On a compass, it is best to do the floating seams so that you can manage the bulk of the seams. This also makes it easier to press your compass flat. But **DO NOT PRESS** until you have added your outside background shape to your compass. The whole compass is made of bias edges, except for the outside background pieces. When cutting, be sure to use grain line arrows.

In the past, quilting has been done both as a necessity and as a decorative touch. It later was considered a hobby and then a craft. Today, it is not only recognized as a money-making craft and business, but, more importantly, as an art.

On the following pages, I have outlined some of the history of the Mariner's Compass. If you would like to learn more, the local libraries in your area can help.

I hope you enjoy and use these patterns for many years to come, for a quilter is someone who is always hungry for new techniques and for what her own imagination can devise by using this new knowledge and taking it beyond the original design.

History of the Mariner's Compass

The Mariner's Compass has been around for as long as people have been traveling the land, going to sea, and drawing maps to follow.

The forerunner of the Mariner's Compass was a stone that was known as a T-0 map, which was divided with a T within a circle. This produced a world divided in half and two quarters: On the half section, east was at the top and represented Asia; the lower left quarter was Europe, and the lower right quarter was Africa. It was not only a map, but it showed the directions of each country in a crude way. Later on, astronomers developed the mathematical expression of direction, but expressing it in universally acceptable terms to all nations was slow in developing. Directions, for the most part, were very limited for the average person. North was toward the darkness, and south was toward the light. Heracleitus had divided the heavens into four quarters: the bear (north), morning (east), evening (west), and the region opposite the bear (south). Besides the stars, it was also natural for the ancients to think of the winds in terms of direction. The winds along with the sun were thought of in terms of good and evil, depending upon the weather they brought. The ancients could only speculate on where the winds came from.

The four winds blew from the north, south, east, and west. The ancients not only gave the stars names but also the four winds, even the winds varying with just a slight degree of direction. The ancients had many options as to how many different winds there were, but Aristotle seems to have been the one to suggest a subdivision of the four chief winds into three parts. Making a wind rose of twelve, the circle of twelve winds was reduced to eight. This theme was carried out in the building of the Tower of Winds at Athens about 100 B.C. The twelve point rose was carried over into the fourteenth century, with variations showing a system of sixteen winds also being used at the same time. Flemish marine mariners of Bruges (Belgium) adapted Frankish (West German) names of the winds. It is noted with a rumor that names of the compass were adopted by the pilots of Bruges. The compass that we know today is a combination of the ancient wind rose and a T-0 map.

Because the ancients divided the circle according to the four winds instead of degrees, even the most untutored knew the winds. At first, medieval compass cords were divided into twelve directional points, then later into eight, representing points N, NE, E, SE, S, SW, W, and NW. Eventually thirty-two points emerged—eight primary winds, eight half winds, and sixteen quarter winds, giving even greater precision. Often the cards were drawn with an artistic flair, reminding sailors of a thirty-two-petaled flower, which later was known as the wind rose.

The wind rose was used mainly as an easy way of dividing the circular horizon. Instead of numbers or degrees of arc, the winds were given names, which was as natural as giving the stars names.

How to Use This Book

Read through the book to familiarize yourself with the instructions and patterns. The first section explains supplies and fabrics. The next section explains and illustrates how to draw an oval and how to make compass points. Study the color photos to decide which shape you would like and if you are going to use the curved seam. You should also decide at this point what item you are going to make—for example, a wall hanging, a purse, a tote bag, a jacket, or a full-sized quilt. The item you are going to make will also determine the number of compasses you will need.

When you have selected the pattern or patterns you will use, the next step is to trace the pattern pieces. If you are doing piece work, there is no need to trace the full compass master draft. But if you are doing applique, you will need to trace the full compass master draft and the pattern pieces, eliminating the background patterns.

If you have a very steady hand, you can lay your template plastic on top of the pattern pieces in the book and eliminate the freezer paper tracing. But if you prefer, you can trace onto the freezer paper first before transferring to template plastic.

Beside each compass master draft, you will find approximate yardage requirements for that compass. I have not given yardage for wall hangings, quilts, etc., because each individual should devise their own layout for their project. If you have problems with layouts, the rectangles can be sewn together like squares to form rows. The hexagons will fit together in the same manner as the Grandmother's Flower Garden pattern. The diamond can also be sewn into diagonal rows or can be sewn in the layout for the Lone Star, the Broken Star, or any number of traditional patterns using the diamond shape.

If you are using solid colors for your compass, the yardage stated beside each compass draft will be enough to produce two to four of that compass. But if you are using a striped or printed fabric of one-way designs to achieve a certain effect, you might need additional yardage. This will depend upon the repeat of the stripe or printed fabric and the size of your item.

If you are not efficient at estimating yardage, don't be concerned. The rule of thumb for any quilter is to buy extra fabric at the time of purchase. If you make a mistake or run out of fabric, it is very difficult to match colors or to find the same print or stripe again. Any fabric left over can always be incorporated into another project.

The patterns for the compasses and hexagon, rectangle, and diamond background all have seam allowances added.

The outside background patterns (on page 102) to be added to the pieced oval have not had seam allowances added. These need to be traced onto your freezer paper first so that you can add seam allowance before doing your plastic template.

Getting Started

To get started, you will need the following list of supplies, some of which you might already have on hand:

DRAWING

- freezer wrap paper (Reynolds)
- lead pencil—.05
- quilter's ruler
- compass protractor
- eraser
- template plastic
- fine-point pen (permanent ink)
- scotch tape
- paper scissors (sharp point)
- string
- heavy map pins

SEWING

- thimble
- needles—no. 9
- thread—regular and quilting
- fabric
- scissors—sewing
- batting
- safety pins
- rotary cutter and mat
- straight pins
- quilting hoop (or floor frame)
- sheet for backing
    (thread count—180)
- bias tape for binding

If you are doing any size square or rectangle up to 12 or 16 inches, the freezer paper may be used right off the roll. If you are doing a Mariner's Compass wider than the freezer paper, you will need to tape two lengths together on the back (shiny side of the paper). Be certain your length is longer than your width, to allow enough space to draw your oval. Also, make notes on color schemes and quilting designs you might want to use.

You can proceed in either of two ways: First draw the oval and proceed to the degree lines; or first do the degree lines and then draw the oval. Both ways are acceptable. Then proceed to draw in your points.

Fabric

I prefer to use cotton/poly fabrics 95% of the time. The other 5%, I use 100% cotton because I cannot get the prints I want to use in cotton/poly.

There are four things that I do not like about 100% cotton, and they are the reasons I use cotton only when necessary:

Cotton SHRINKS: usually it will shrink completely on the first or second washing. But I have seen cotton shrink again after a third or tenth washing of a finished quilt.

Cotton BLEEDS: depending upon the dye color, cottons will bleed onto other lighter colors, even after three or more washings of a finished quilt.

Cotton WRINKLES and RAVELS: when cotton is washed, it wrinkles; needless to say, it has to be pressed. Cotton also ravels, which means you must be careful how you handle it.

Cotton FADES: cottons will fade from exposure to the sun, even in diffused light, dry cleaning solvents, and even some detergents, depending upon the dye color.

The choice of fabric is yours. Just remember, always wash it before using, even the cotton/poly.

I also experiment with other fabrics. If I see a print or design in something considered "not for quilting," I buy 1/8 to 1/4 yard. I then cut 1/4 or 1/2 of it off and wash it. Most of the time, I know it will shrink; but, that's okay, as long as the surface is not marked. Once a fabric is washed, you will be able to determine if it is suitable to use.

I also use cotton/poly sheets on the backs of my wall hangings and quilts. However, I use only sheets that are 180 thread count. A higher count is too tight to quilt, and a lower count is too loose. By using sheets, I have no seams on the back. Before washing the sheet, take out the hems on the top and bottom.

Drafting Techniques

There are many different ways to draw an oval. One is to find an object in the shape of an oval and trace around it, then proceed to draw in the points. The second is to use an old-fashioned method, that is, with string and pins along with a compass. The third is using a ruler, compass, and a straight, firm strip of paper.

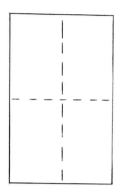

Figure 3.1

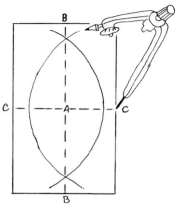

Figure 3.2

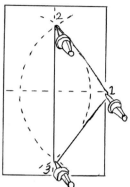

Figure 3.3

DRAWING METHOD I

You already have your vertical and horizontal lines which divide your paper into fourths. (See Fig. 3.1.) Now, determine the length and width you want your compass to be.

Using a compass, place the point of the compass on center point "A," and open it until it reaches either the top or bottom (horizontal length) on either your 90-degree point or line "B." This will give you the set width between compass lead and point.

Without changing the compass, place the point now on (vertical width) "O" degree or line "C," and make a semi-circle. Next, place the point on the opposite side and distance of center point "A" and make another semi-circle. (See Fig. 3.2.)

If you do not have a compass, or if you are drawing a large compass, the pencil, string, and map pin will work.

Mark the place where the two semi-circles intersect with either a letter or number (I have used numbers). Now place pins at 1, 2, and 3. (See Fig. 3.3.)

Tie a string around the three map pins tightly so that there is no slack. Do not pop pins out by tying too tightly.

Remove pin 1 and replace it with a pencil. (See Fig. 3.4.) Keeping the string taut, pull the pencil around the pins to draw an oval. (See Fig. 3.5.)

To make a smaller-size oval in the center, draw a small rectangle the size you wish for the center, and follow the same steps used for the outside oval shape.

Now you are ready to draw in your points.

With this method, you can only estimate the size you want. If you are designing the complete quilt top to make your own patterns, this method will work well for you.

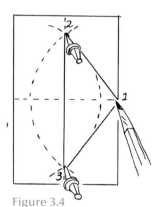

Figure 3.4

Figure 3.5

DRAWING METHOD II

Here is a simple geometrical method of making ovals to fit any desired space:

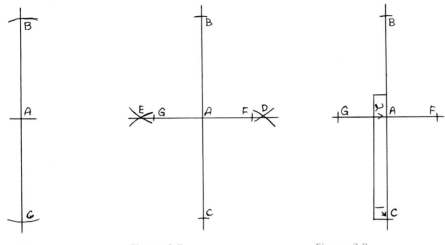

Figure 3.6   Figure 3.7   Figure 3.8

Draw a straight line the length of, or longer than the desired length of the oval. At the center of the line, establish point "A." With the compass, swing arcs to points "B" and "C," oval length. (See Fig. 3.6.)

From "B" and "C," swing arcs above and below line "BC." Connect their intersections with line "DE." On this line, mark points "F" and "G" equal distances from "A" to establish the width of the oval. (See Fig 3.7.)

Mark points "1" and "2" to match "A" and "C" on a straight, firm strip of paper. (See Fig. 3.8.)

Turn this measuring paper vertically along line "FG" so that point "1" is at "F." Mark point "3" at "A." (See Fig. 3.9.)

Rotate the measuring paper clockwise, moving point "3" along line "AC" and point "2" along "AG." Make dots opposite point "1." Connect these dots with a line that completes the first quarter of the oval. Repeat this procedure in the other three parts or make a tracing and transfer curve to complete the oval. (See Fig. 3.10.)

This method is best used when you want to insert a compass into an open space of an existing pattern.

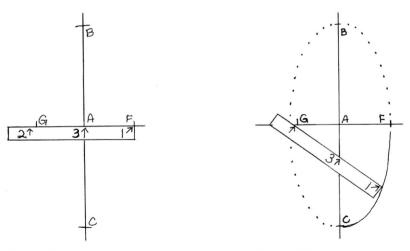

Figure 3.9   Figure 3.10

Folding, Drawing, and Marking Points

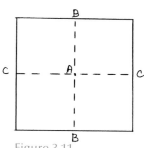

Figure 3.11

FOLDING—METHOD 1

Starting with a sheet of paper (size will depend upon how large a compass you are drafting), you will first fold it in half, crease, open, and fold in half again, crease, until you have folded the paper into even fourths. Completely unfold that sheet of paper. Now mark your center as "A," the vertical fold as "B," and the horizontal fold as "C." Now take a ruler and pencil and draw lines "B" and "C" from edge to edge of the paper. (See Fig. 3.11.) Fold the paper in half diagonally, crease both ways to form an "X" on the paper. Open and mark lines "D" (left top to bottom right) and "E" (right top to bottom left). (See Fig. 3.12.)

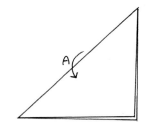

Figure 3.12

Fold line "B" over to line "D" to form the line "F," crease. Next, fold line "C" over to line "D" to form the line "G" crease. Open and mark lines "F" and "G." Do each full half so that each 1/4 section is folded and marked. (See Fig. 3.13.)

You now have a square that has been folded into sixteenths and forms your sixteen points of the compass. Always remember that point "A" is in the center.

After marking all your degree lines, you can now press your paper on the back to flatten it out before you proceed. This makes it easier to draw in the actual sides of each point. If using freezer paper, press on the side you are drawing.

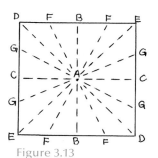

Figure 3.13

FOLDING—METHOD 2

Fold a sheet of paper in half and half again. Crease folds both ways. Open up and mark vertical and horizontal lines. These will form your "0°" and "90°" lines.

Draw in these lines with your ruler. Be very accurate. Now, with a protractor lined up on the horizontal "0°" line, you will find your other degree (or points) lines, marking off at "22°," "45°," "68°," etc., all around the paper. After the top half is marked, turn your paper around, line up the protractor on line "0°" again, and continue to mark the rest of the degrees. Now, with a ruler and pencil, draw in your lines, connecting each degree as shown. This forms the basis on which you will form your points. (See Fig. 3.14.)

I have already drawn in the ovals so you will have a better understanding of what I mean in relation to the paper edges. (See Fig. 3.14.)

No matter whether an oval or circle, the same folding and degree method is used to achieve equal divisions.

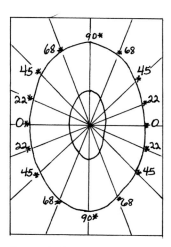

Figure 3.14

Now that you have sixteen divisions and your oval drawn, we proceed to draw in the points.

It is understandable, when working with a miniature oval compass, that there is no way you can achieve a compass with thirty-two or sixty-four points that would be comfortable to work with, considering it would have such small pieces. It's just too small, and you would have too many seam allowances on the back to be able to quilt through.

This section will show you how to achieve your sixteen points, whether you are working with a miniature or a full-size compass. A miniature will have no more than sixteen points, but on a full-size compass, you can keep expanding to the outer edge of the quilt if desired.

First, you have to decide what you want your center to be: a diamond, circle, octagon, or square. There is no set size for the center, unless you are using patterns from this book.

You may want to experiment to find the proportions of whatever center you have decided upon. Just remember, the smaller the diamond, circle, oval, octagon, or square in the center, the thinner the points of the star will be.

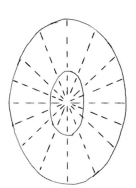

Figure 3.15

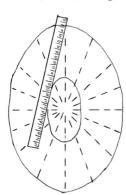

Figure 3.16

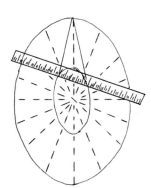

Figure 3.17

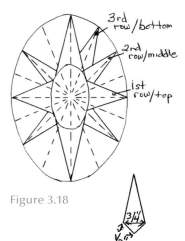

Figure 3.18

Figure 3.19

Figure 3.15 shows what your compass will look like at this point with the center drawn in. Figure 3.16 indicates placing a ruler edge at the outside oval at the "90°" point aligned with the inside oval at the "45°" point to form the left side of the north point. Repeat on the right side. Figure 3.17 demonstrates the same thing for the east point, using the outside oval point "0°" aligned with the inside "45°" point to form the left side of the east point. Repeat for the right side of the point.

Repeat the same technique until you have the four main points drawn in (north, east, south, west). Proceed to draw in the next four points (second row—NE, SE, SW, NW), which the outside oval point is "45°" point. Figure 3.18 shows how to then proceed onto the next points (third row—NNE, SSE, SSW, NNW).

The majority of the time, the center will determine the base width of the points, especially when working with miniatures. If you come up with your own center, in order to make sure the width at the base (see Fig. 3.19) of your points are uniform all the way out, use these steps.

Figure 3.20

Decide on the width of your four main points. In Figure 3.20, I'm using the Mariner's Compass—North Star. In this compass, I'm using the four main points as a star for my center. After it is drawn in, you now determine the width of your point. The only rule that applies is that your center design should always be the *main focal point*.

The width of the north star is 3/4 inch wide at the base of the point in the center. So that I have an even fraction to work with, I used 1/2 inch for the short or inside edge; you have four outer points ("A," "B," "C," and "D") and four indented points ("E," "F," "G," and "H"). You will measure 1/2 inch out on both sides of each indented point.

For the north point, align your ruler on "90°" (outer edge) and your tick mark on the indented edge of the star, and draw in the lines. Continue until you have all four points of the second row drawn. Proceed to the third row, using the same procedure as for the second row. When the third row is drawn in, your pattern should be complete.

Now decide if you want your points be all one piece or split. Then you are ready to make your templates.

Compass Reference

On the following pages, you will find all sixteen compasses. (Figures 4.1–4.16.) The purpose of these illustrations is to allow you to view them together to see their differences. *They are only for reference.*

These compasses are just a sample of all the possibilities that exist. There are other possible patterns, depending upon a person's imagination. The possibilities are unlimited:

- You can change the centers.
- You can change the points, add or subtract.
- You can also change the background shapes.

Just remember that with each change you make, you will have to do a good bit of redrafting.

Each compass contained within this book will have patterns for all four shapes—oval, hexagon, rectangle, or diamond.

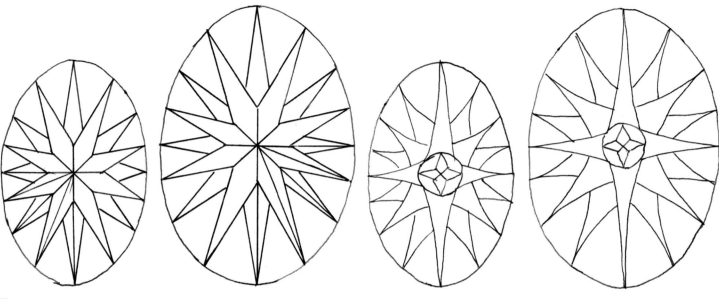

Figure 4.1
Star Ablaze I

Figure 4.2
Star Ablaze II

Figure 4.3
Nova Star I

Figure 4.4
Nova Star II

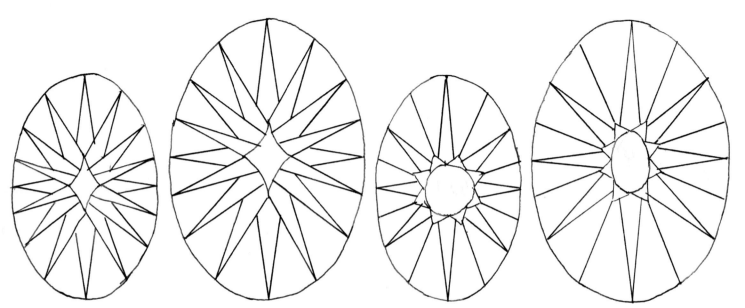

Figure 4.5
Diamond Crystals Star I

Figure 4.6
Diamond Crystals Star II

Figure 4.7
Octad Star L

Figure 4.8
Octad Star II

Figure 4.9
Cameo Star I

Figure 4.10
Cameo Star II

Figure 4.11
Morning Star I

Figure 4.12
Morning Star II

Figure 4.13
Evening Star I

Figure 4.14
Evening Star II

Figure 4.15
North Star I

Figure 4.16
North Star II

In Fig. 4.17, I have chosen Diamond Crystals to show you what one design will look like with all the optional block shapes from which to choose. All sixteen patterns have this option.

Figure 4.17

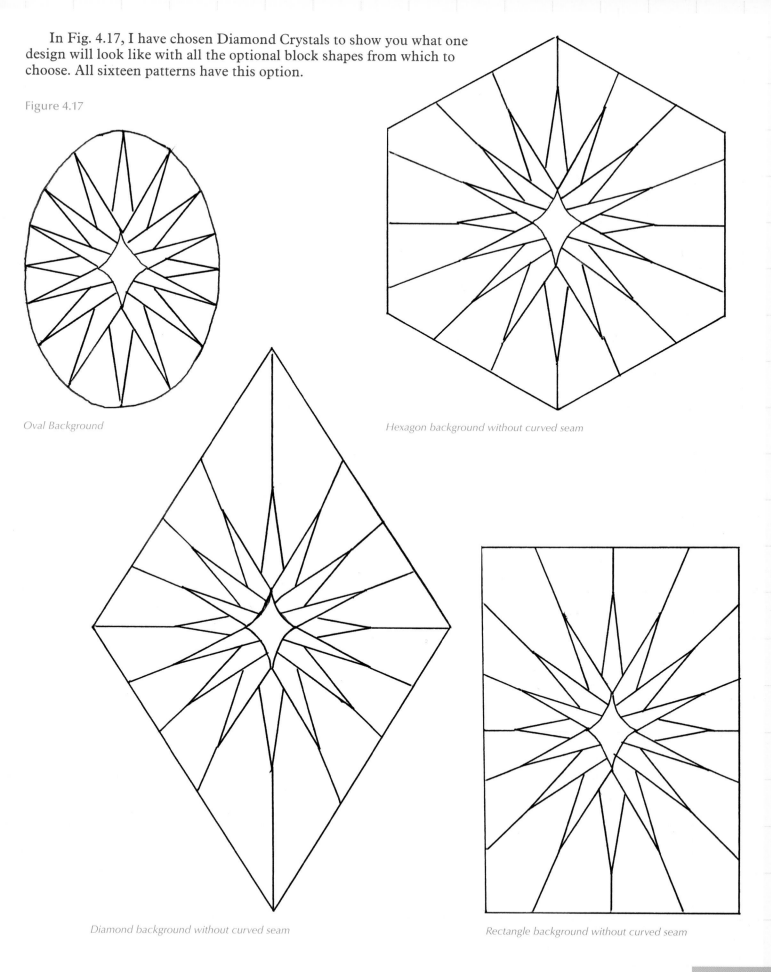

Oval Background

Hexagon background without curved seam

Diamond background without curved seam

Rectangle background without curved seam

Cutting Fabric

All fabric should be washed as soon as you get home with it. If using cottons, you should remove it from the dryer while it has just a slightly damp feel to it so that it will be easier to press out the wrinkles. When pressing your cotton to remove any wrinkles, DO NOT STRETCH your fabric. If you stretch your cotton fabric while pressing, this will eliminate your shrinkage.

If using cotton/poly, you do not need to press. You may use this material as soon as you remove it from the dryer.

If using solid colors or prints with which you don't need to be careful of the design, I suggest that you create four layers with your fabric. Place the template down and cut. With this method, you are cutting your piece and reverse piece at the same time. Referring to the assembly page for the compass you are making, lay out your cut pieces according to figure in the upper left corner. This will show you the exact position for your pieces and reverse pieces.

Pin in position on a piece of freezer paper or a piece of fabric.

Once all the pieces of the block are cut, laid out, and pinned in place, refer to the same assembly page for the sewing sequence.

Assembly and Construction

When doing a Mariner's Compass, the most important thing to remember is that the construction is completely opposite of any other block you have put together.

The secret to piecing is not really a secret. It is a simple, logical sequence. Some squares are put together top row to bottom row, or side row to side row. With the compass, you have to start from the outside edge and work toward the center. One other distinction of the compass is that even though the grain of fabric is used, 95% of the edges are on the bias edge for the patterns in this book. Accuracy is very important in all aspects of quilting, but more so when working with bias edges. This is one reason that some compasses bubble up in the center, even after pressing. Another distinction is pressing as you go. Since you are working with bias edges, do not press with an iron until you have your rectangle, hexagon, or diamond block sewn.

When you start pressing, you will start from the back, always using the steam portion on your iron. The steam helps to bring your bias back into shape. Once you have your seams slightly pressed to lay flat, turn your compass over. Be sure your seams underneath are laying flat, then press the top.

Of the sixteen compasses contained here, all but two have sixteen points. Those two have only eight points each, but the sequence will be the same. Some of the compasses have eight main points, and the others have four main points. Still, the sequence will almost always be the same.

Figure 6.1

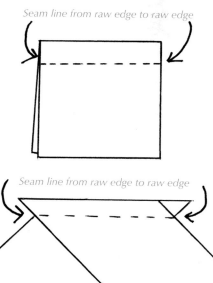

Seam line from raw edge to raw edge

Seam line from raw edge to raw edge

Figure 6.2

Stop sewing line ¼ inch from raw edge. This enables you to set-in the next piece.

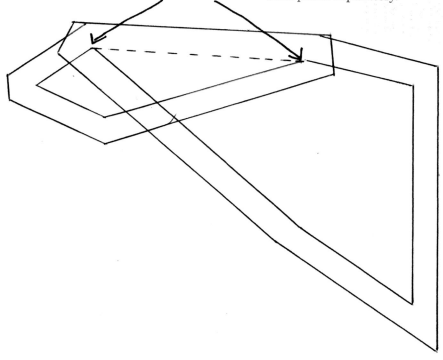

The hardest part of a compass is making certain you have your pieces laid out properly. This will be accomplished if you lay the pieces down in proper position as you cut. With these compasses, you have either mirrored images or reversed pieces, depending upon your terminology. Both are correct. You will also want to use a piece of freezer paper or piece of fabric to pin your fabric pieces to as you lay them out. This will ensure that your pieces do not get misplaced or a breeze of any kind does not misplace them.

If you are using split points, these need to be sewn together first, depending upon which compass you are using. On other compasses, the split points aren't joined until you sew together the four quarters into a whole.

When you begin sewing your pieces together, you will sew from raw edge to raw edge. (See Fig. 6.1.) But you will also have floating seams to enable you to join your background pieces at the end of each point together without the seam twisting. Floating seams will also be used when setting in your 1/4 sections. (See Fig. 6.2.)

When you look at the patterns, you will see that you have four background outside edges for your block from which to choose. (See Fig. 4.17.)

For those who want the curved edge, but would still like to use a rectangle, hexagon, or diamond background block edge, you have that choice.

For those who do not want a curved seam, I have eliminated it. You choose the appropriate background patterns for whichever shape you desire.

You also have the option of using lattice stripping if you so desire.

Also, for those quilters who like to applique only, every one of these patterns may be completed in Celtic design techniques with bias tape. You also have the choice of cutting the compass as a whole compass or cutting each point separately.

Tips for Piecing

BE ACCURATE: in any successful piecing, you must be as accurate as possible.

BIAS EDGE: be very careful NOT to stretch bias edges while sewing and pressing.

GRAIN LINE ON PATTERN: be sure to follow the grain line on pattern pieces. This is one of the tricks to piecing a successful compass.

MARKING SEAM LINES: after making your templates, to ensure accuracy, take a straight pin, heat the tip, and make a hole in your template at sewing line angles large enough for the pencil lead to touch fabric to mark the point. (See Fig. 7.1.)

FLOATING SEAMS: make sure you remember where your floating seams need to be.

PRESSING: never use your iron to press until you have completed your compass block. Use the steam setting.

Figure 7.1

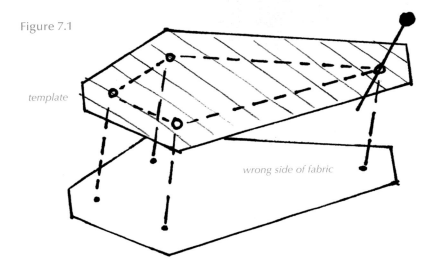

template

wrong side of fabric

Patterns

With these compasses, I have given the individual the choice of using the curved seam or not, and still be able to choose from three outside block shapes.

On the following pages, you will find a full-side draft plus pattern pieces for each compass. You will also find patterns for different backgrounds. You may do an oval and then still choose from three outside background shapes—hexagon, rectangle, or diamond on fold-out pages in back.

Or you may choose to eliminate the curved oval seam; if so, when choosing your background patterns, you still may choose one of the three shapes—hexagon, rectangle, or diamond.

On the following compass master drafts for each pattern, you will see an oval dash line. This dash line represents the original oval shape with which I started to draft these patterns.

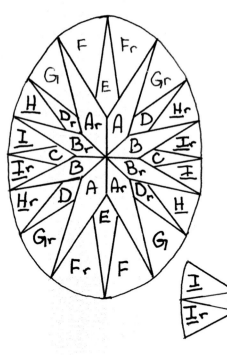

1. Sew G and H pieces to corresponding sides of D. Sew all four sections.

2. Sew F pieces to corresponding sides of E. Sew both sections.

3. Sew I pieces to corresponding sides of C. Sew both sections.

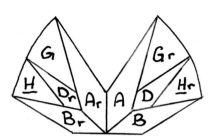

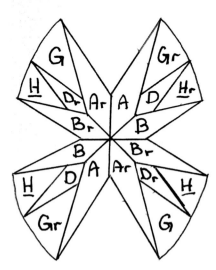

4. Sew A and B pieces to corresponding sides of G-D-H sections. Sew all four sections.

5. Sew two 1/4 sections together to form half. Repeat for other two 1/4 sections.

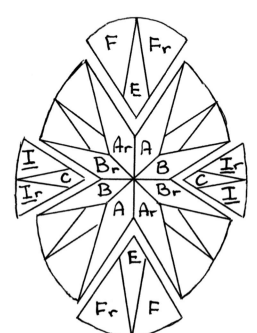

6. Sew two halves together.

7. Sew sections F-E-F and I-C-I to main compass section with the set-in method to complete compass.

1. STAR ABLAZE I
MASTER DRAFT

FABRIC:

1/8 yd- 1st row
1/8 yd- 2nd row
1/2 yd- background

CUT:
(r = reverse)

Solid points:

A- 2
Ar- 2
B- 2
Br- 2
C- 2
D- 2
Dr- 2
E- 2

Split points:

Aa- 4
Aar- 4
Ba- 4
Bar- 4
Ca- 2
Car- 2
Da- 2
Dar-2
Db-2
Dbr-2
Ea- 2
Ear-2

Backgrounds:

F- 2
Fr-2
G- 2
Gr-2
H- 2
Hr- 2
I- 2
Ir- 2

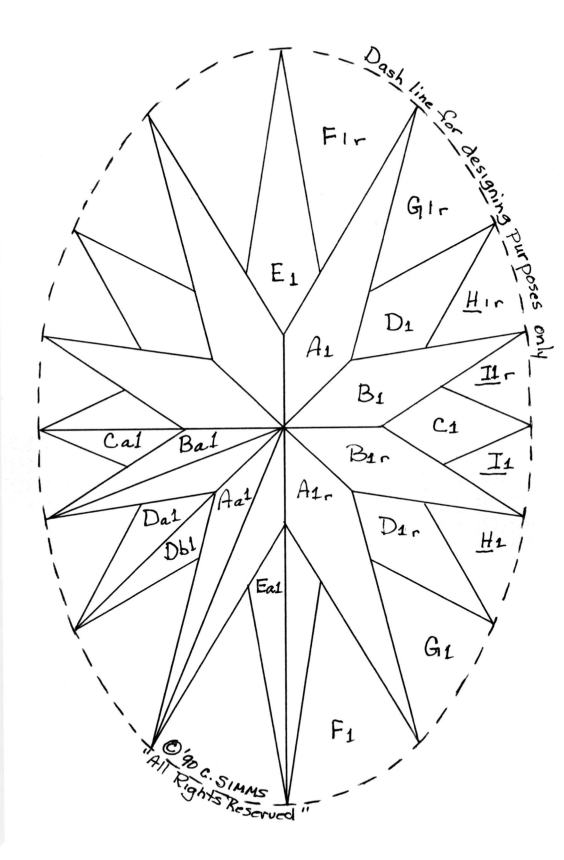

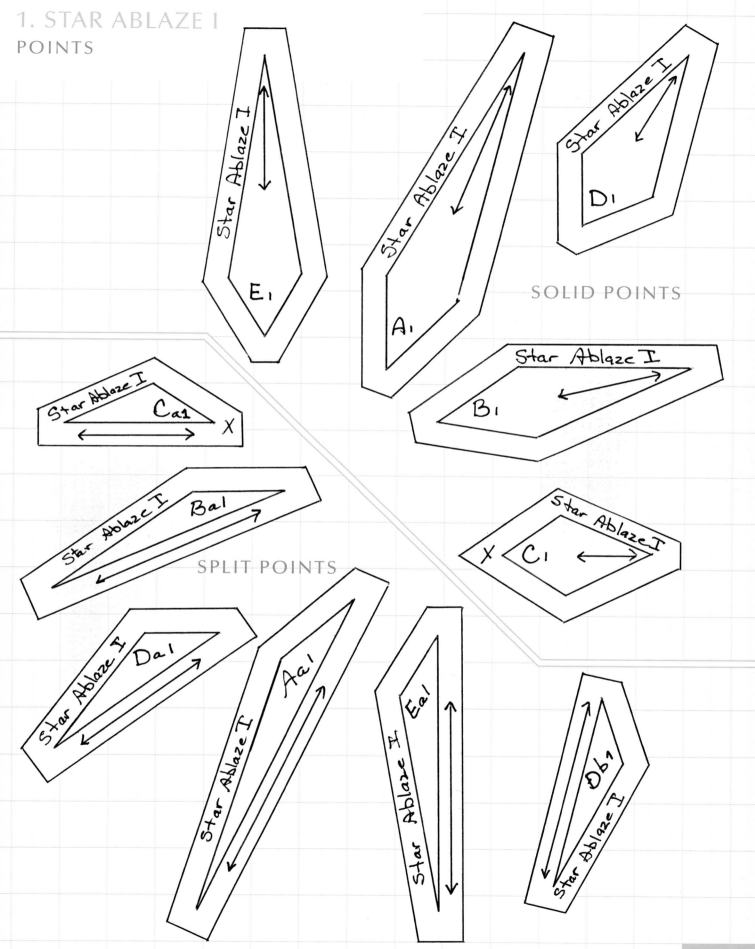

SOLID POINTS

SPLIT POINTS

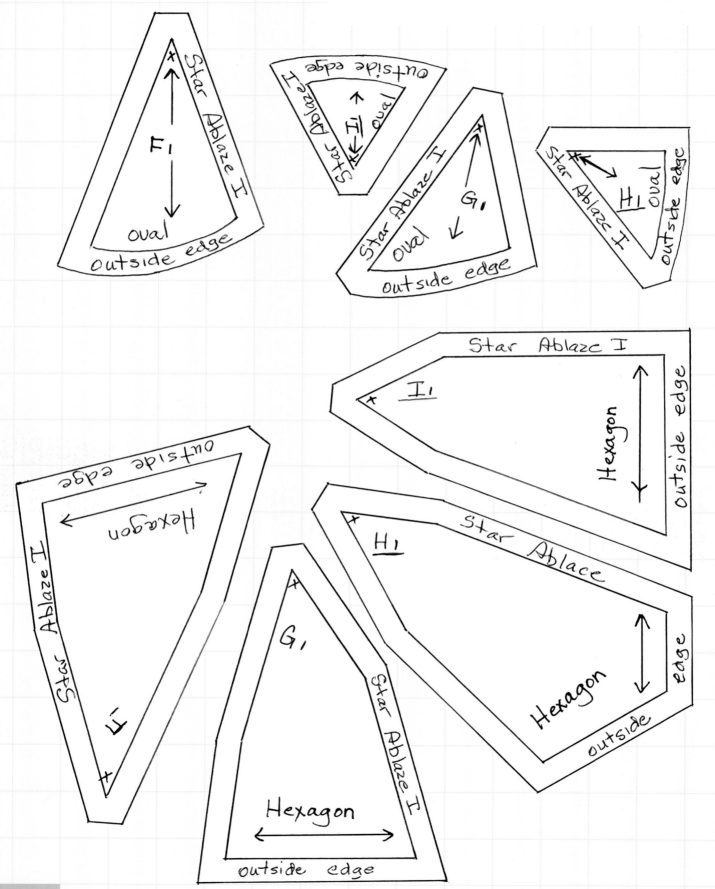

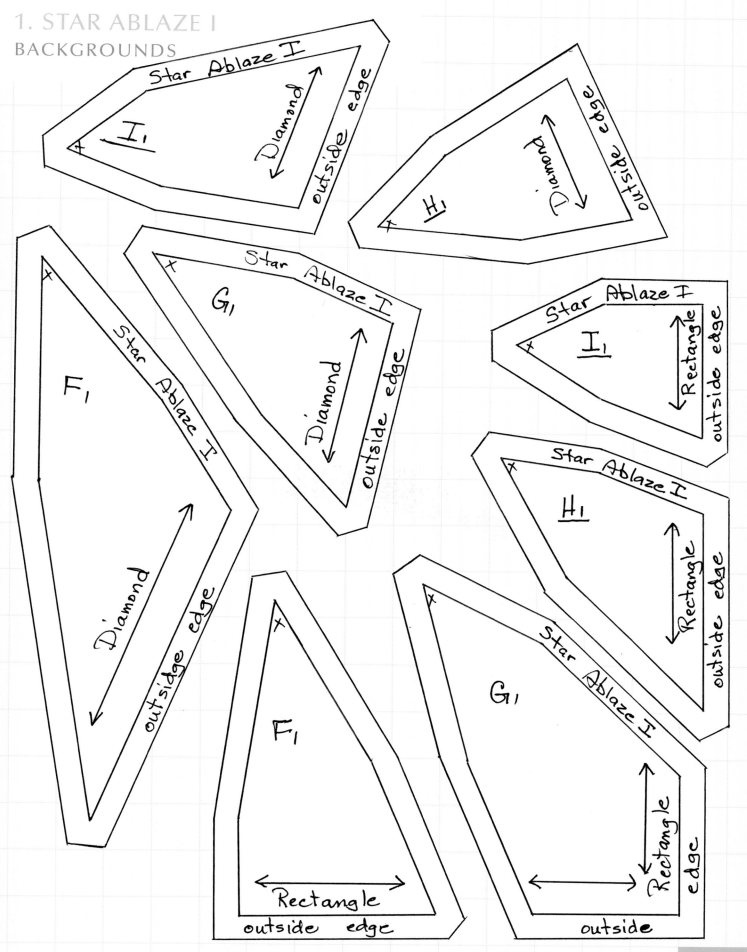

2. STAR ABLAZE II
MASTER DRAFT

FABRIC:

1/4 yd- 1st row
1/4 yd- 2nd row
3/4 yd- background

CUT:
(r = reverse)

Solid points:

A- 2
Ar- 2
B- 2
Br- 2
C- 2
D- 2
Dr- 2
E- 2

Split points:

Aa- 2
Aar- 2
Ab- 2
Abr- 2
Ba-2
Bar- 2
Bb-2
Bbr-2
Ca-2
Car-2
Da-2
Dar-2
Db-2
Dbr-2
Ea-2
Ear-2

Backgrounds:

F- 2
Fr- 2
G-2
Gr- 2
H- 2
Hr- 2
I-2
Ir-2

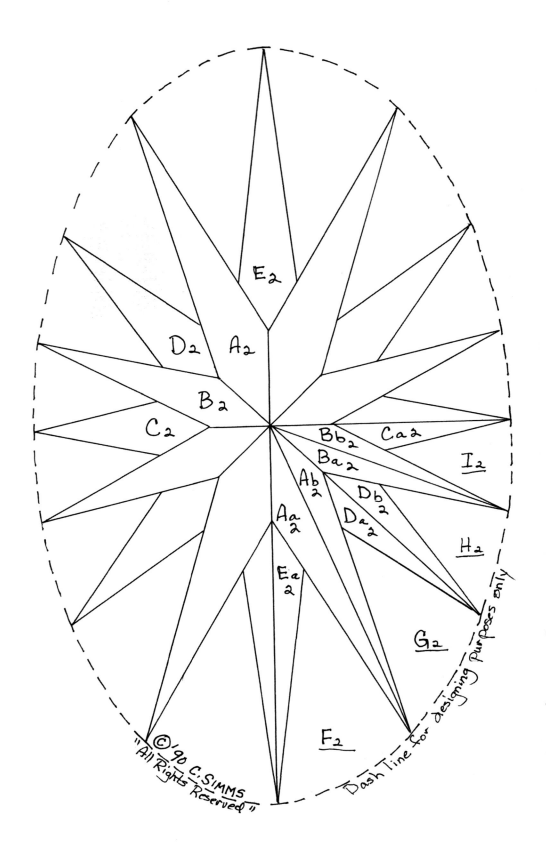

Dash Line for designing purposes only

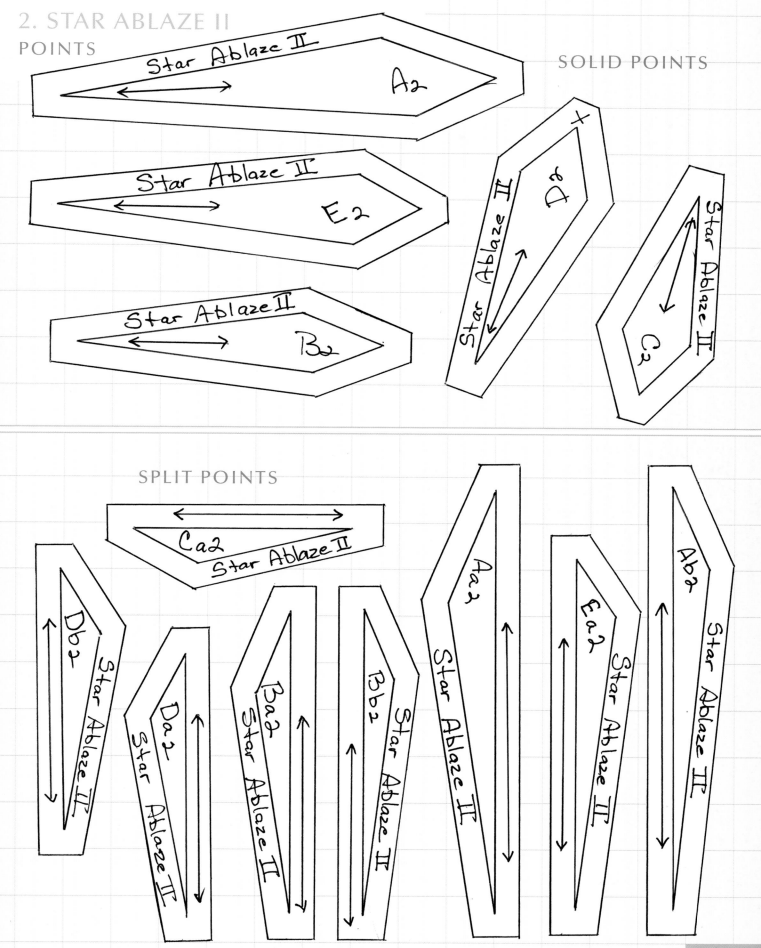

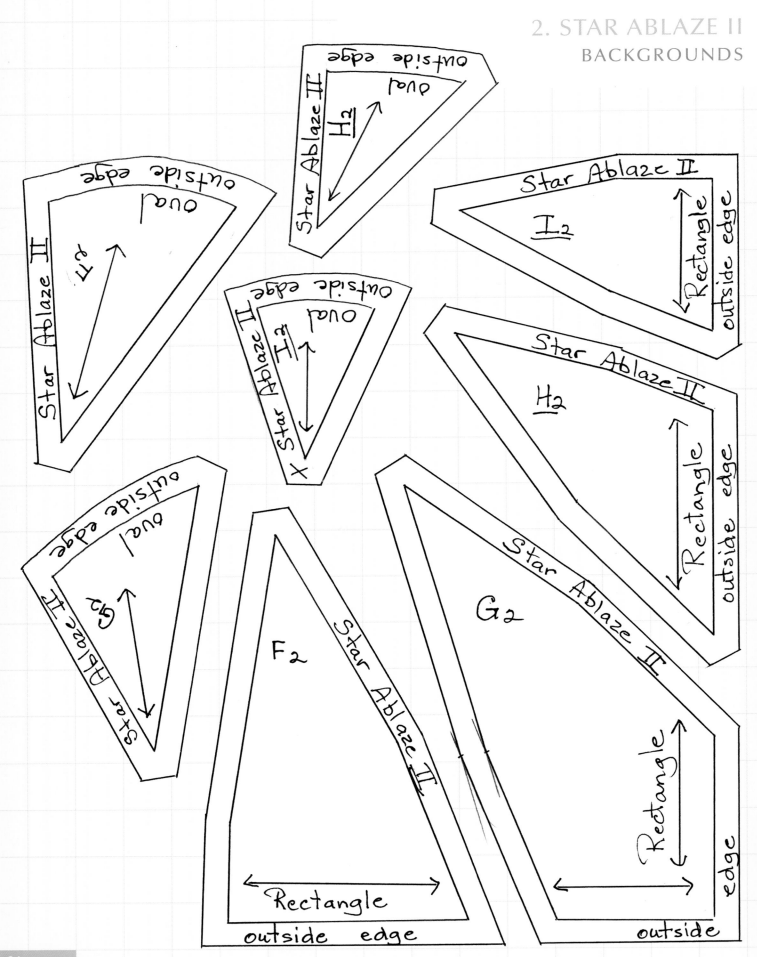

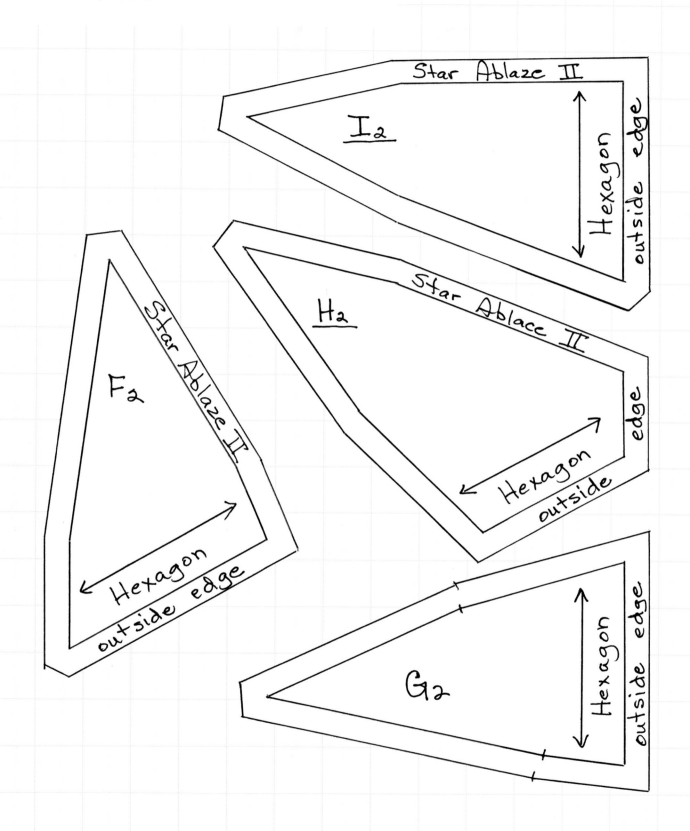

Star Ablaze II

I₂

Hexagon outside edge

Star Ablaze II

F₂

Hexagon outside edge

H₂

Star Ablace II

Hexagon outside edge

G₂

Hexagon outside edge

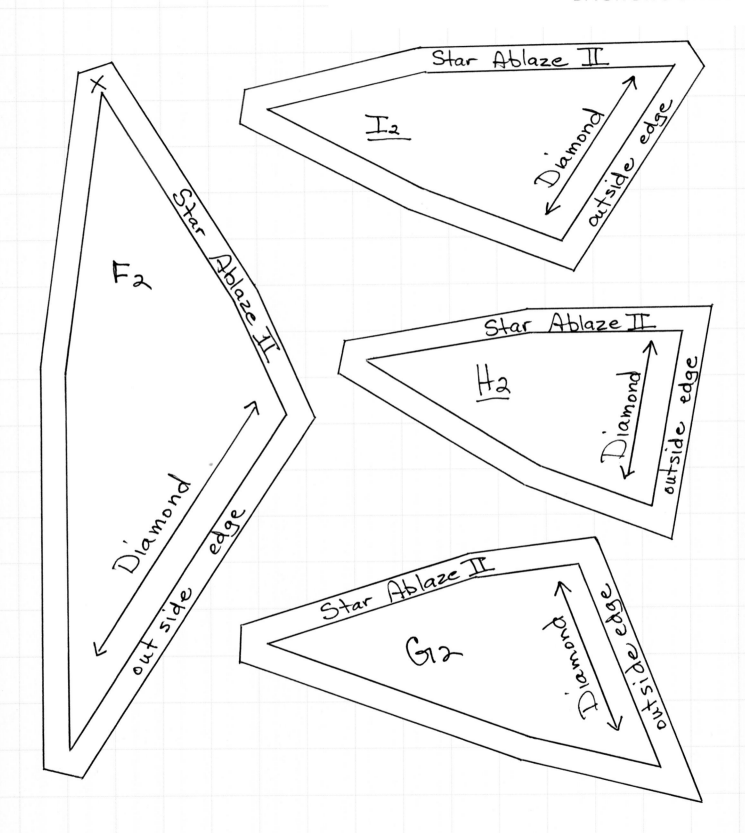

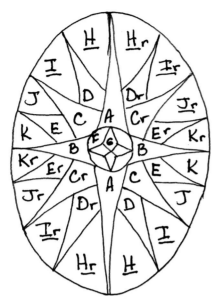

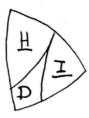

1. Sew H and I pieces to corresponding sides of D. Sew all four sections.

2. Sew J and K pieces to corresponding sides of E. Sew all four sections.

3. Join G pieces together to form star.

Set in F pieces to form circle.

4. Sew H, D, I and J, E K sections to corresponding sides of C. Sew ll four sections.

5. Sew A and B pieces to corresponding sides of H, D, I C, J, E, K section. Join to circle.

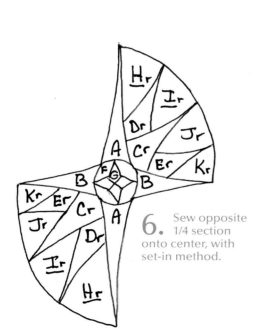

6. Sew opposite 1/4 section onto center, with set-in method.

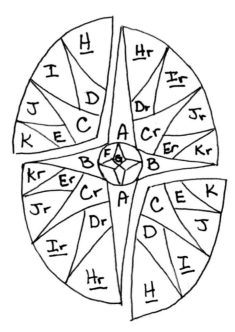

7. Sew in remaining 1/4 sections to main compass section with the set-in method to complete the compass.

FABRIC:

1/8 yd- 1st row
1/8 yd- 2nd row
1/8 yd- 3rd row
1/2 yd- background

CUT:
(r = reverse)

Points:

A-2
B-2
C-2
 Cr-2
D-2
 Dr-2
E-2
 Er-2

Center:

F-4
G-4

Backgrounds:

H-2
 Hr-2
I-2
 Ir-2
J-2
 Jr-2
K-2
 Kr-2

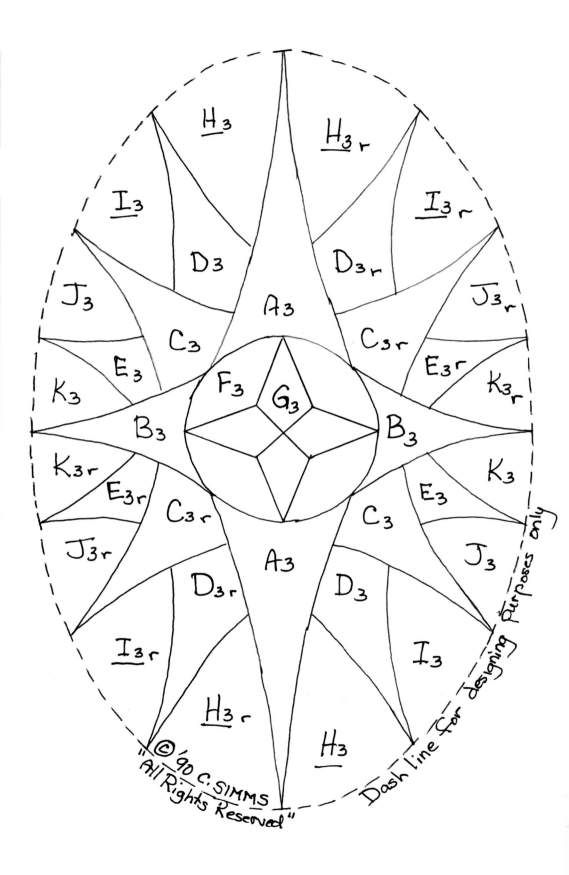

Dash line for designing purposes only

3. NOVA STAR I

POINTS / CENTER / BACKGROUNDS

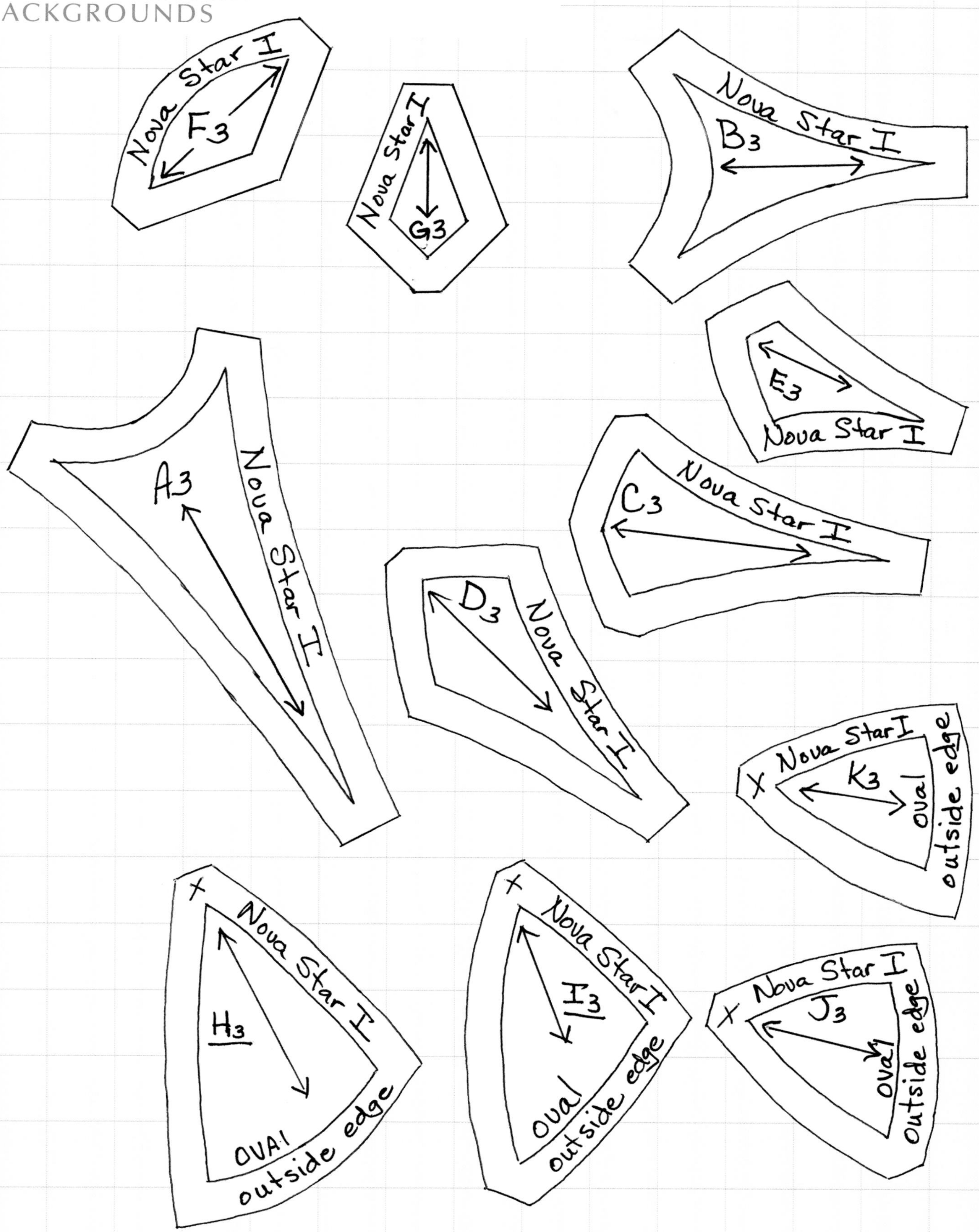

Nova Star I
F3
Nova Star I
G3
Nova Star I
B3
E3
Nova Star I
Nova Star I
A3
Nova Star I
C3
D3
Nova Star I
Nova Star I
K3
oval
outside edge
Nova Star I
H3
oval
outside edge
Nova Star I
I3
oval
outside edge
Nova Star I
J3
oval
outside edge

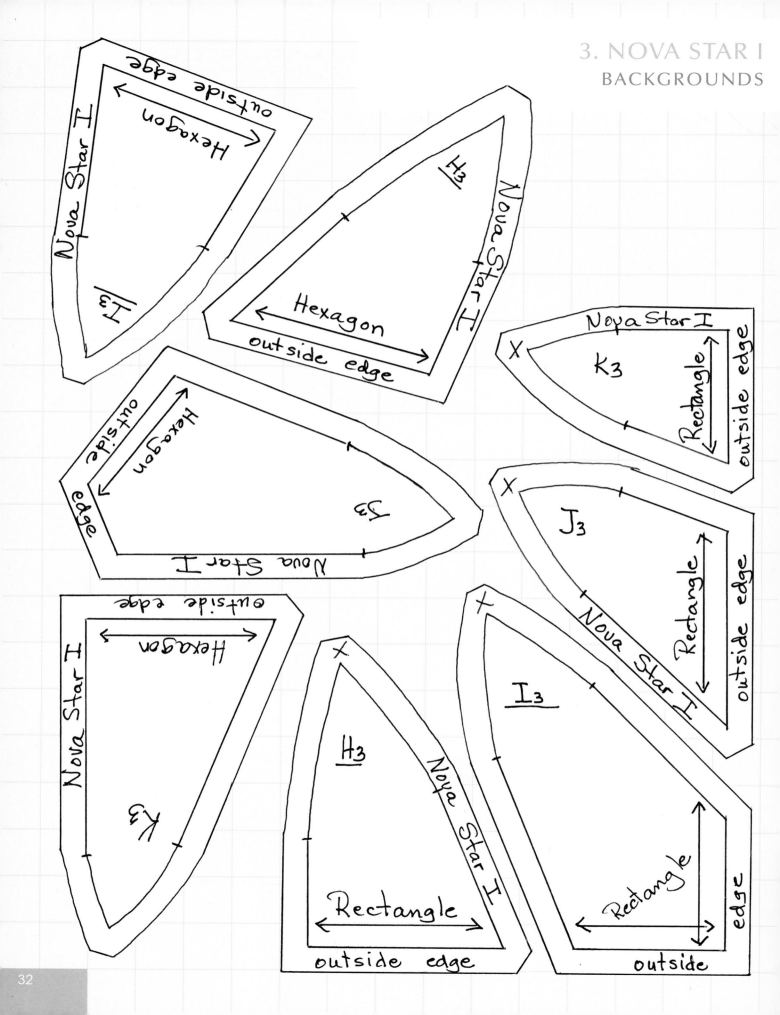

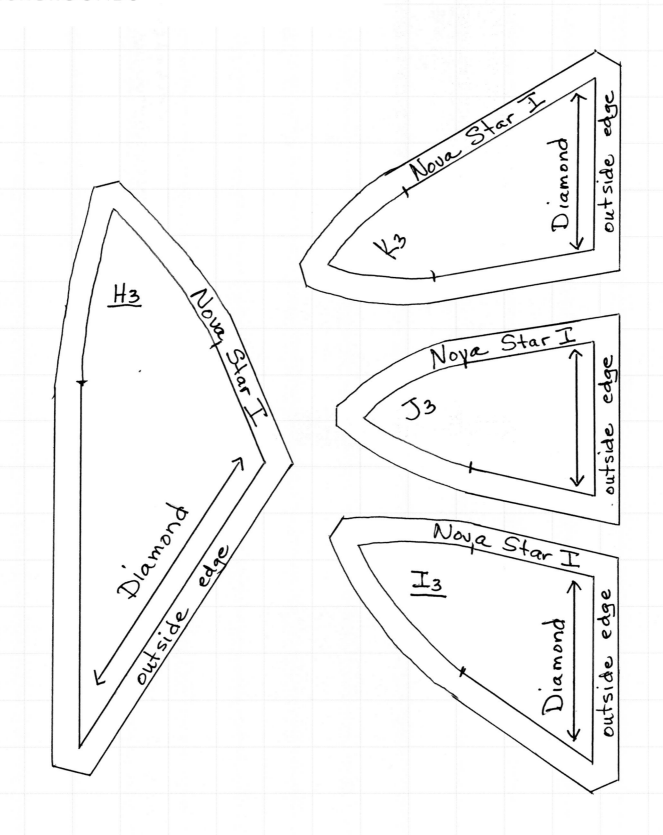

4. NOVA STAR II
MASTER DRAFT

FABRIC:

1/4 yd- 1st row
1/4 yd- 2nd row
1/4 yd- 3rd row
3/4 yd- background

CUT:
(r = reverse)

Points:

A- 2
B- 2
C- 2
 Cr-2
D- 2
 Dr- 2
E- 2
 Er-2

Center:

F-4
G-4

Backgrounds:

H- 2
 Hr- 2
I- 2
 Ir- 2
J- 2
 Jr- 2
K- 2
 Kr-2

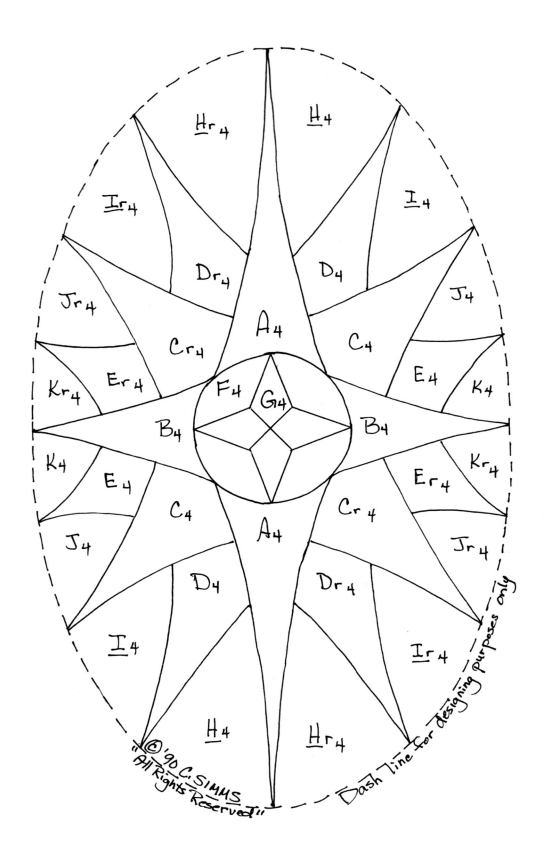

Dash line for designing purposes only

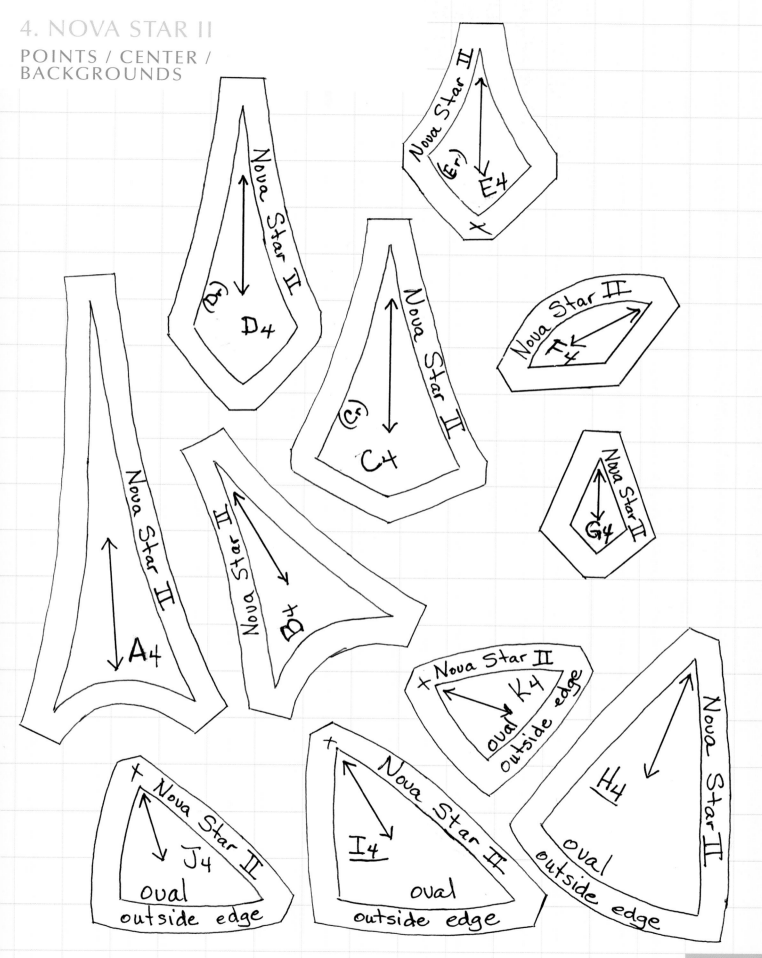

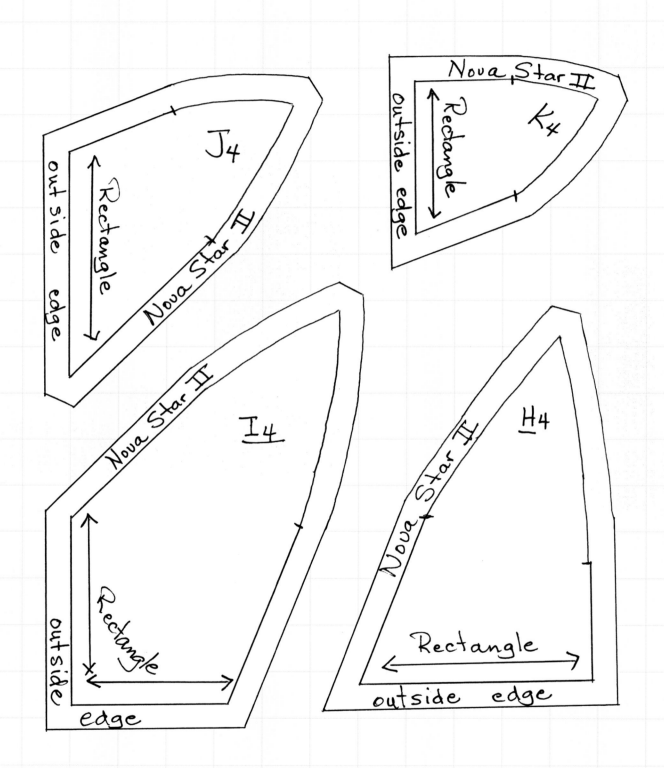

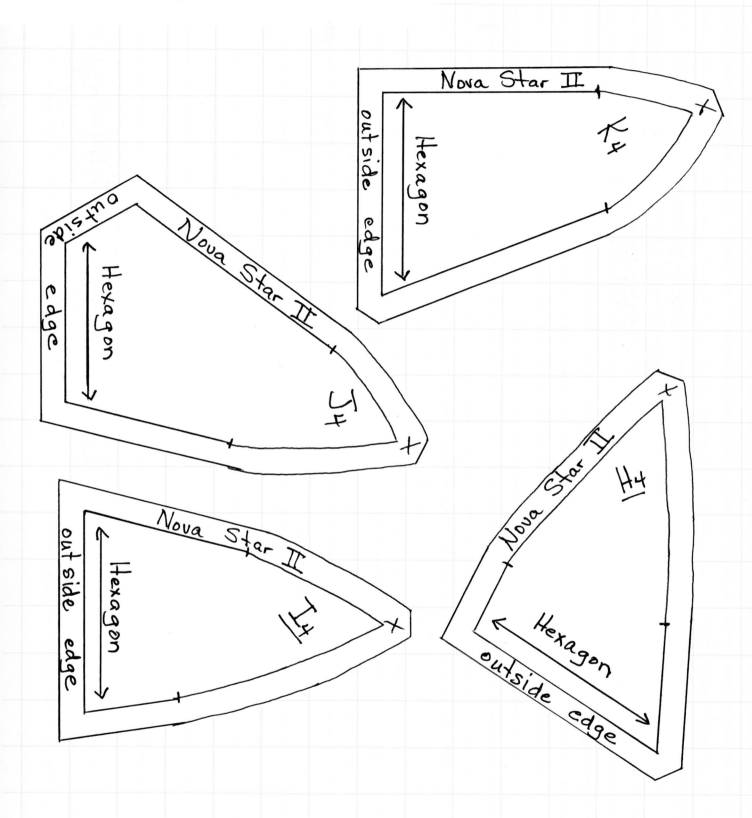

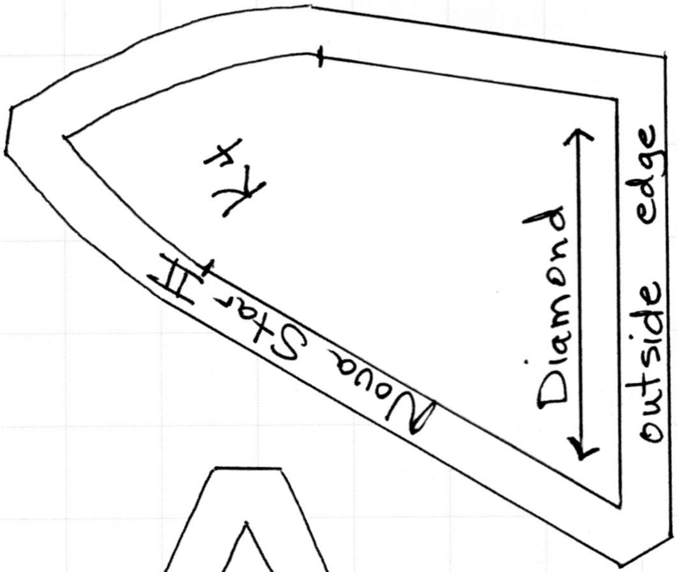

Nova Star II
K4
Diamond
outside edge

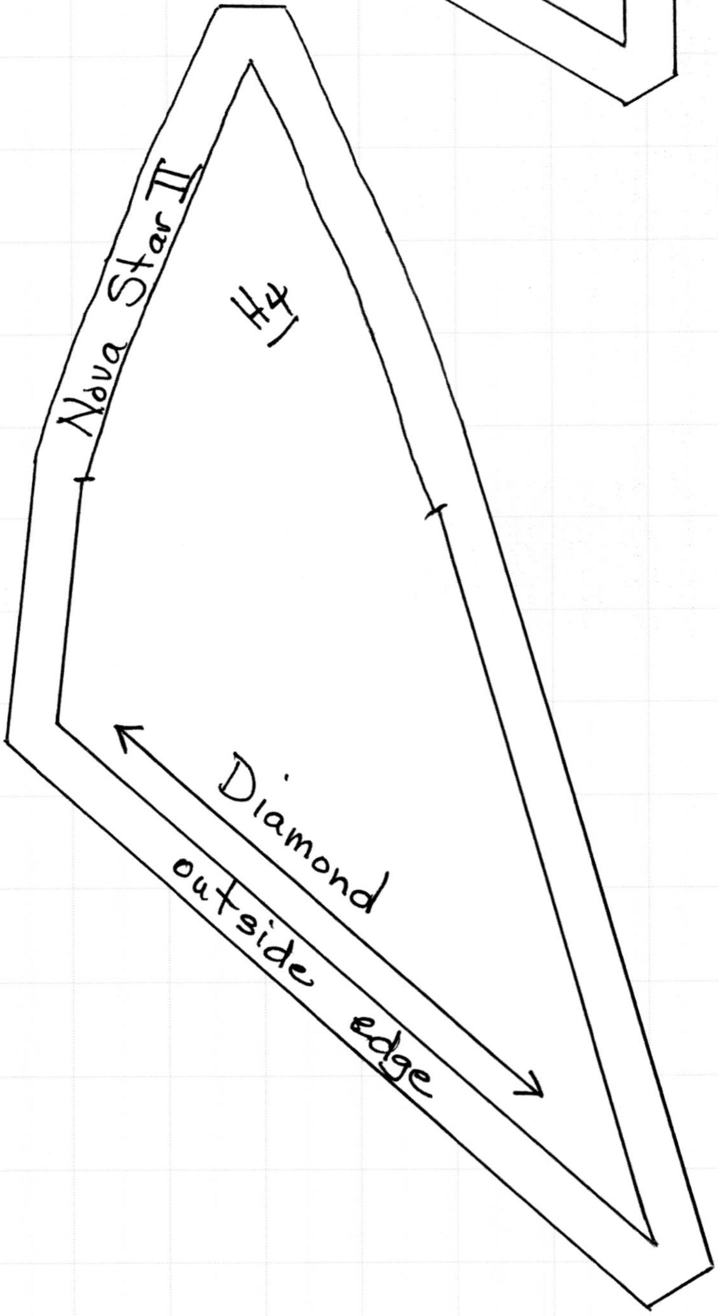

Nova Star II
H4
Diamond
outside edge

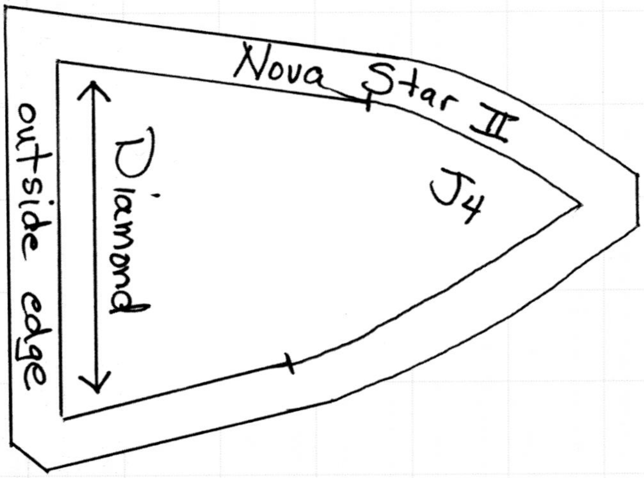

Nova Star II
J4
Diamond
outside edge

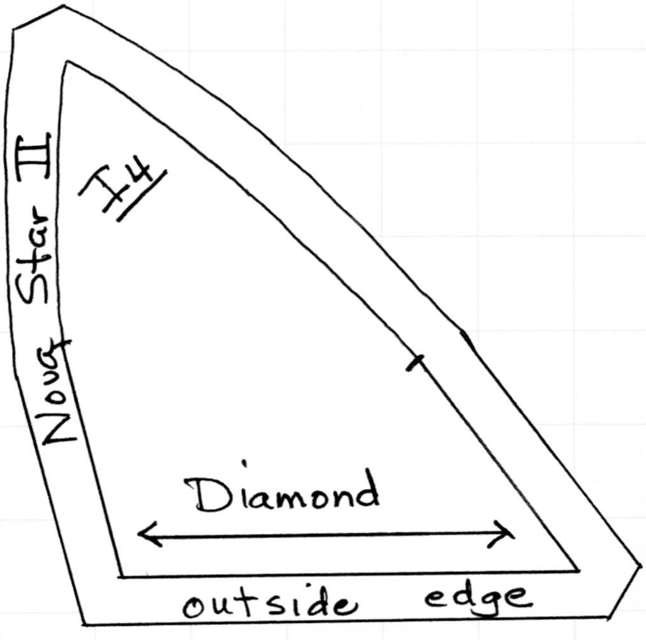

Nova Star II
H4
Diamond
outside edge

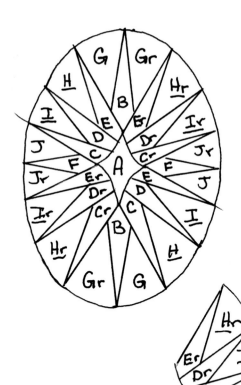

1. Sew G and Gr pieces to corresponding sides of B. Sew both sections.

2. Sew J and Jr pieces to corresponding sides of F. Sew both sections.

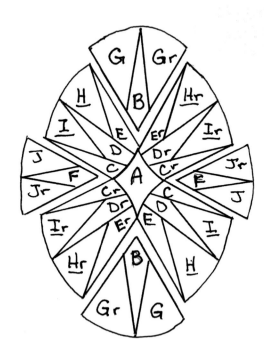

3. Sew Hr (H) to corresponding side of Er. Sew Dr to corresponding side of E-H. Sew Ir to corresponfing side of Dr. Sew Cr to corresponding side of Dr and Ir. Sew all four sections.

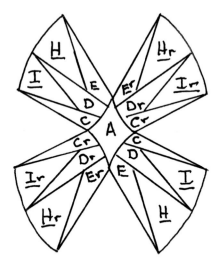

4. Sew each E-H-D-I-C section to corresponding sides of diamond.

5. Sew both sections G-B-Gr Sew both sections J-F-Jr Then sew sections to main compass with the set-in method.

5. DIAMOND CRYSTALS STAR I
MASTER DRAFT

FABRIC:

1/8 yd- B, F points
1/8 yd- D points
1/8 yd- C, E points
1/2 yd- background
center- any of the
above fabrics or scrap

CUT:
(r = reverse)

Center:

A-1

Solid Points:

B- 2
C- 2
 Cr- 2
D- 2
 Dr- 2
E- 2
 Er- 2
F- 2

Split Points:

Ba- 2
Bar- 2
C1- 2
 Car- 2
Cb- 2
 Cbr- 2
Da- 2
 Dar- 2
Db- 2
 Dbr- 2
Ea- 2
 Ear- 2
Eb- 2'
 Ebr- 2
Fa- 2
 Far- 2

Backgrounds:

G- 2
 Gr- 2
H- 2
 Hr- 2
I- 2
 Ir- 2
J- 2
 Jr- 2

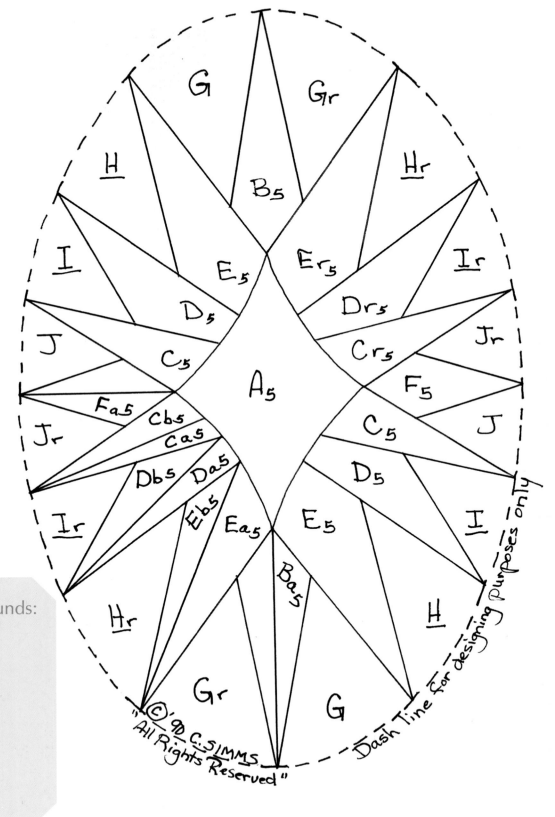

Dash line for designing purposes only

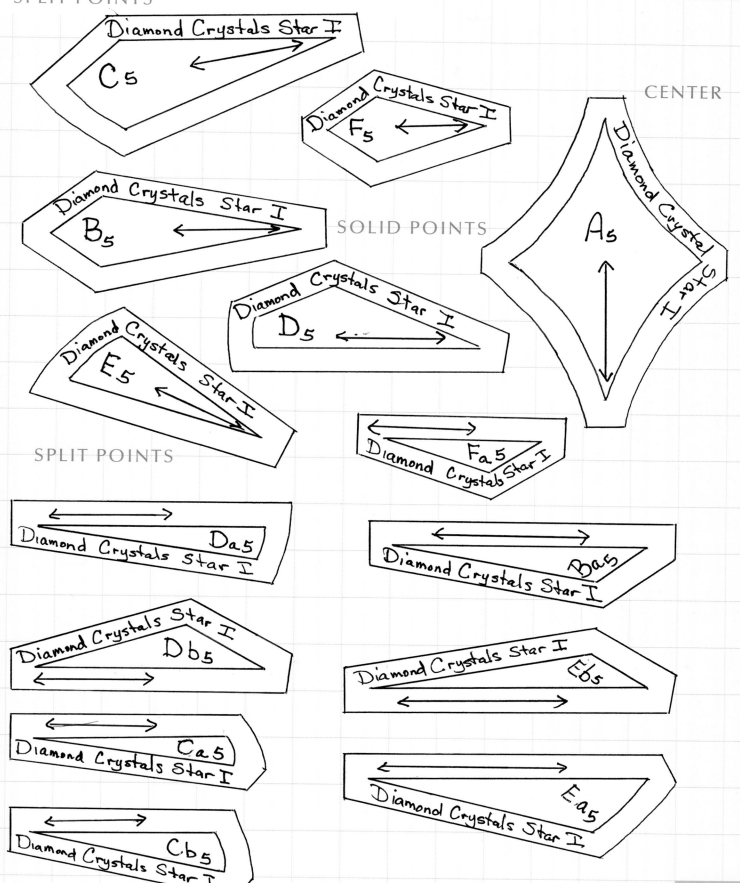

Diamond Crystals Star I — C5

Diamond Crystals Star I — F5

CENTER

Diamond Crystals Star I — A5

Diamond Crystals Star I — B5

SOLID POINTS

Diamond Crystals Star I — D5

Diamond Crystals Star I — E5

SPLIT POINTS

Diamond Crystals Star I — Fa5

Diamond Crystals Star I — Da5

Diamond Crystals Star I — Ba5

Diamond Crystals Star I — Db5

Diamond Crystals Star I — Eb5

Diamond Crystals Star I — Ca5

Diamond Crystals Star I — Ea5

Diamond Crystals Star I — Cb5

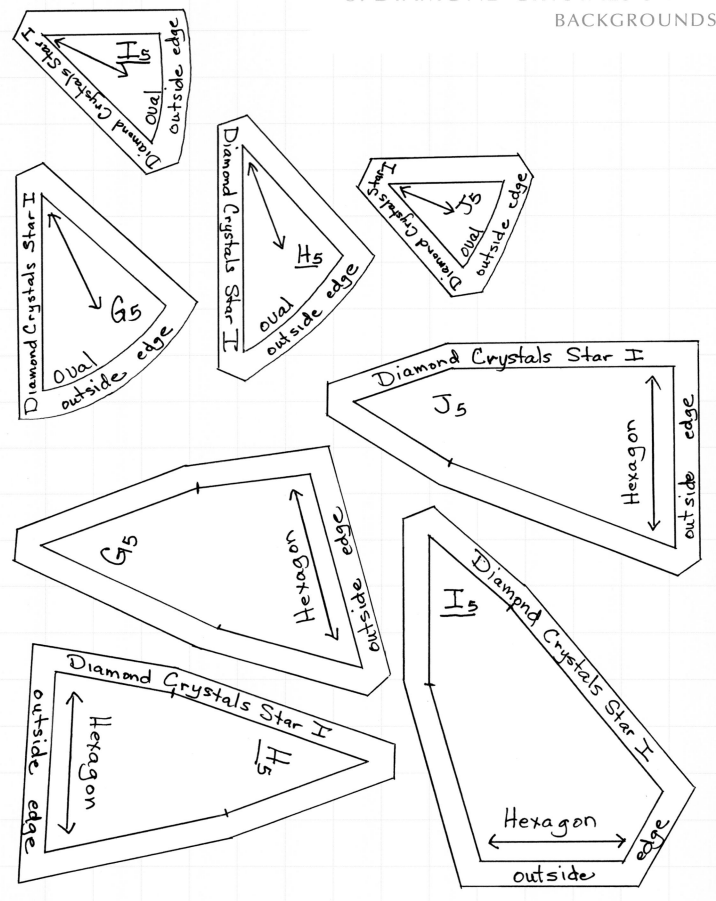

Diamond Crystals Star I — I5 — Oval — outside edge

Diamond Crystals Star I — G5 — Oval — outside edge

Diamond Crystals Star I — H5 — Oval — outside edge

Diamond Crystals Star I — J5 — Oval — outside edge

Diamond Crystals Star I — J5 — Hexagon — outside edge

Diamond Crystals Star I — G5 — Hexagon — outside edge

Diamond Crystals Star I — I5 — Hexagon — outside edge

Diamond Crystals Star I — H5 — Hexagon — outside edge

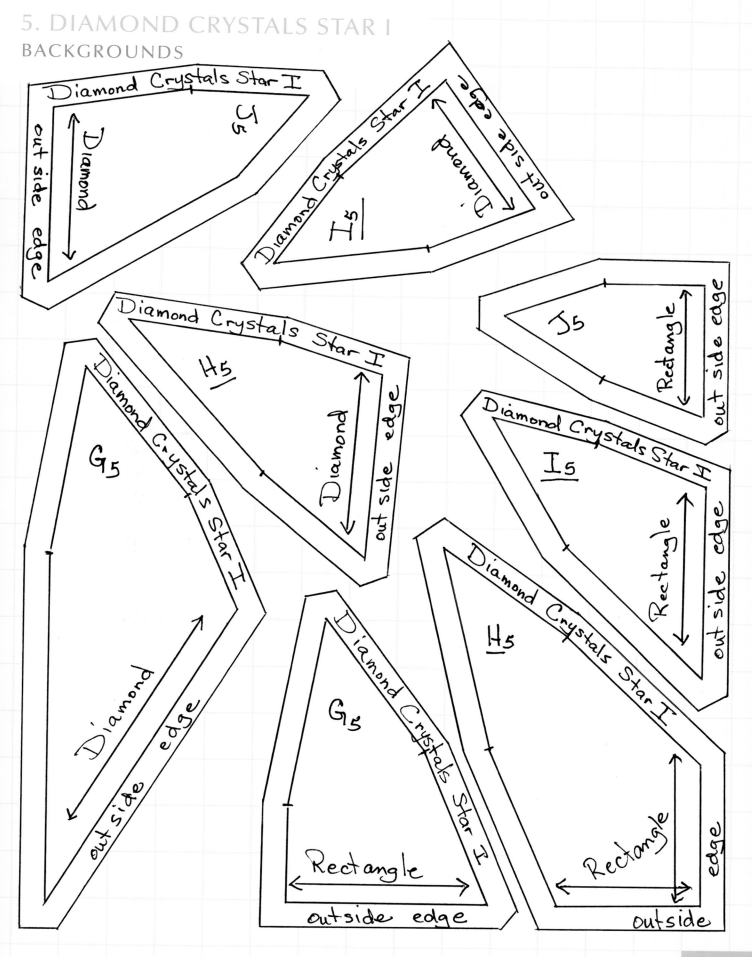

6. DIAMOND CRYSTALS STAR II
MASTER DRAFT

FABRIC:

1/4 yd- B, F points
1/4 yd- D points
1/4 yd- C, E points
3/4 yd- background
center- any of the
above fabrics or scrap

CUT:
(r = reverse)

Center:

A-1

Solid Points:

B-2
C-2
 Cr- 2
D- 2
 Dr-2
E-2
 Er- 2
F- 2

Split Points:

Ba- 2
 Bar- 2
Ca- 2
 Car- 2
Cb- 2
 Cbr- 2
Da- 2
 Dar- 2
Db- 2
 Dbr- 2
Ea- 2
 Ear- 2
Eb- 2
 Ebr- 2
Fa- 2
 Far- 2

Backgrounds:

G- 2
 Gr-2
H- 2
 Hr-2
I- 2
 Ir- 2
J- 2
 Jr- 2

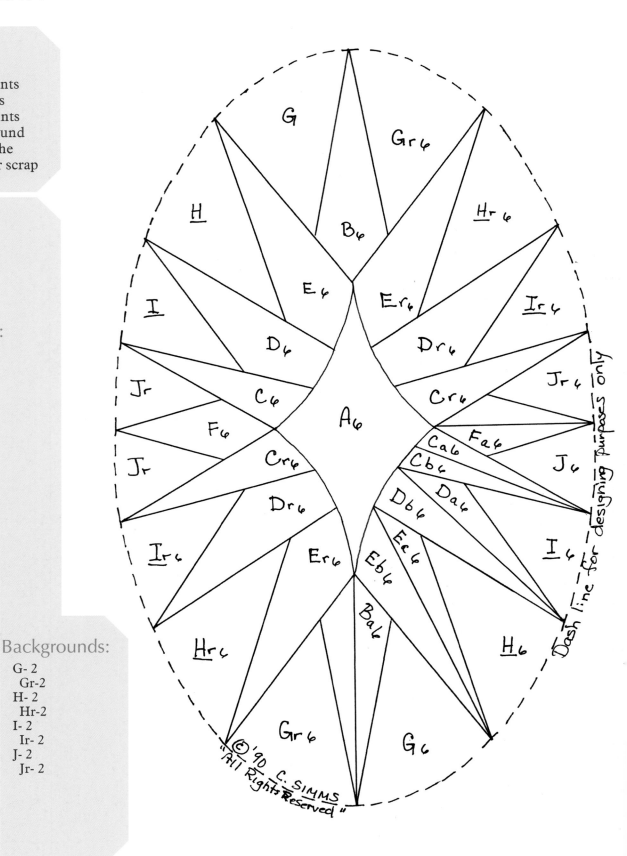

CENTER

SOLID
POINTS

SPLIT POINTS

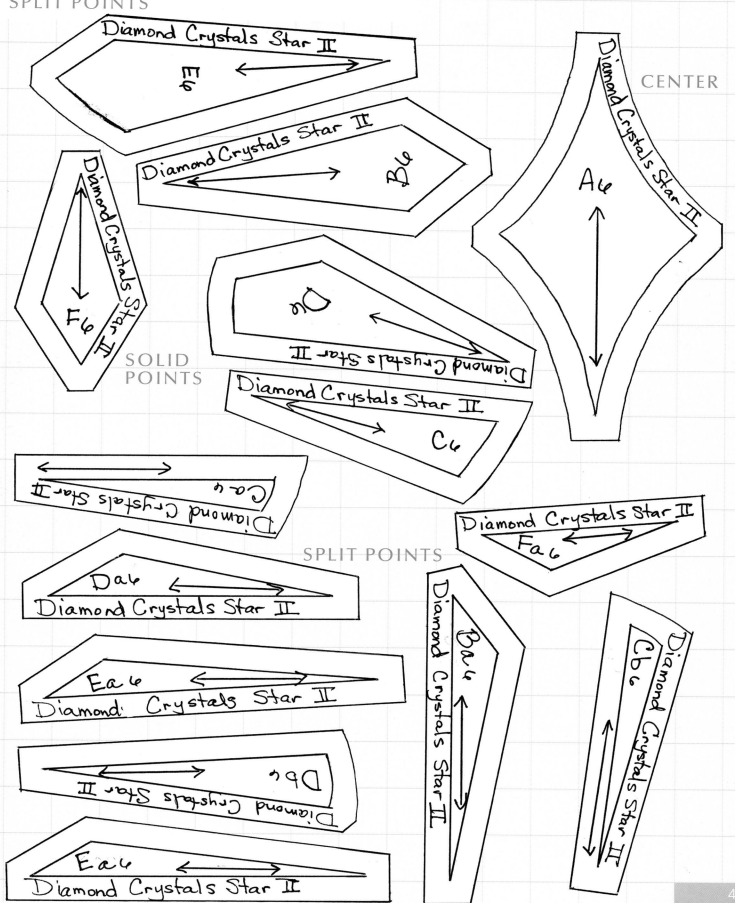

Diamond Crystals Star II — E6

Diamond Crystals Star II — B6

Diamond Crystals Star II — A6

Diamond Crystals Star II — F6

Diamond Crystals Star II — D6

Diamond Crystals Star II — C6

Diamond Crystals Star II — Ca6

Diamond Crystals Star II — Fa6

Diamond Crystals Star II — Da6

Diamond Crystals Star II — Ea6

Diamond Crystals Star II — Db6

Diamond Crystals Star II — Ba6

Diamond Crystals Star II — Cb6

Diamond Crystals Star II — Ea6

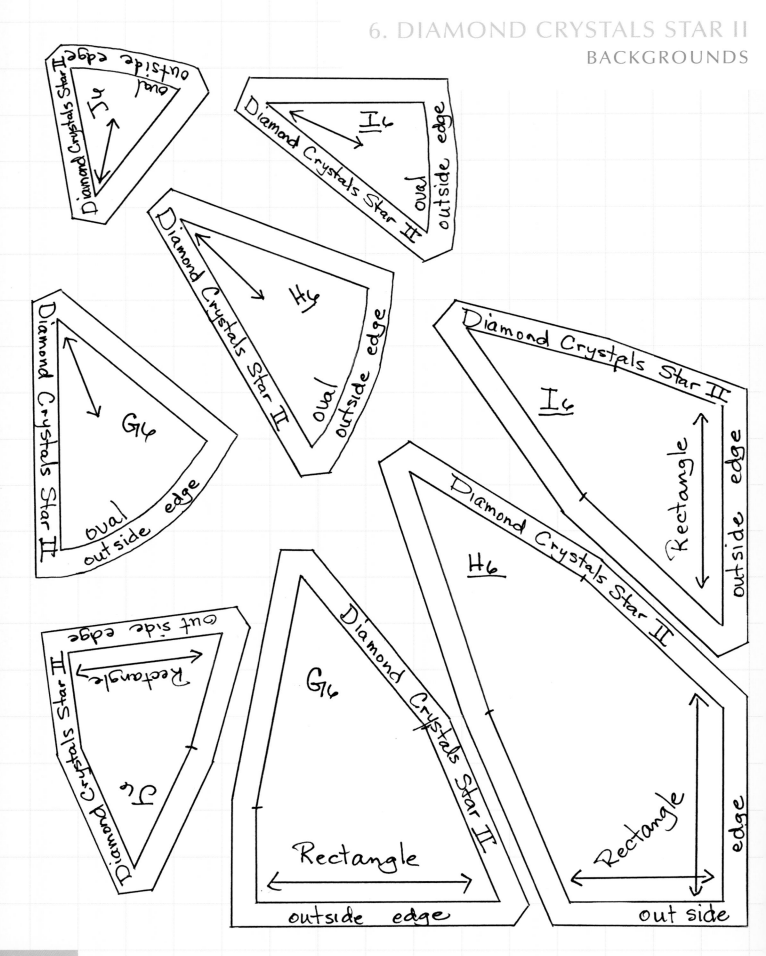

Diamond Crystals Star II J6 oval outside edge

Diamond Crystals Star II I6 oval outside edge

Diamond Crystals Star II H6 oval outside edge

Diamond Crystals Star II G6 oval outside edge

Diamond Crystals Star II I6 Rectangle outside edge

Diamond Crystals Star II H6 Rectangle outside edge

Diamond Crystals Star II J6 Rectangle outside edge

Diamond Crystals Star II G6 Rectangle outside edge

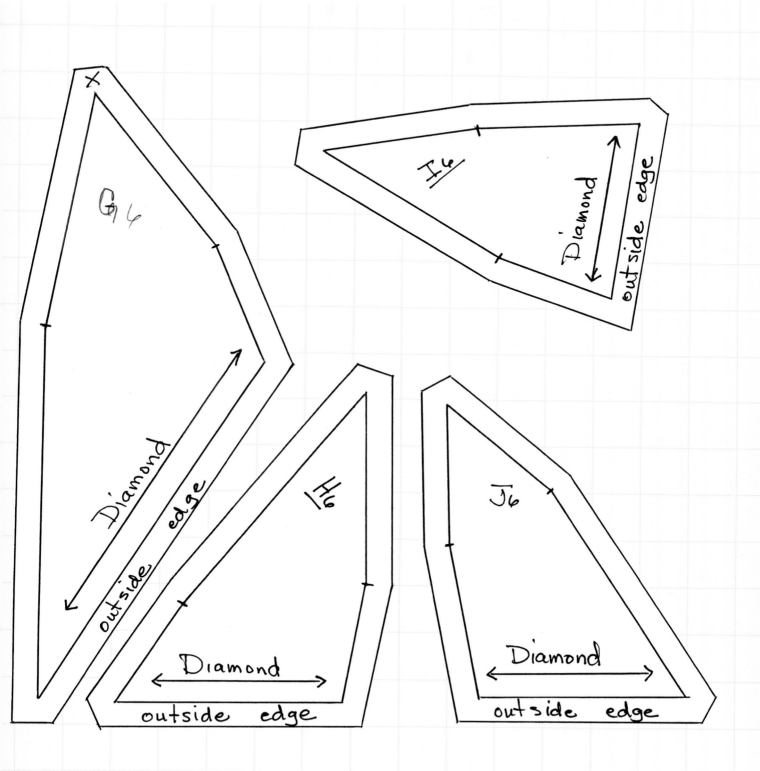

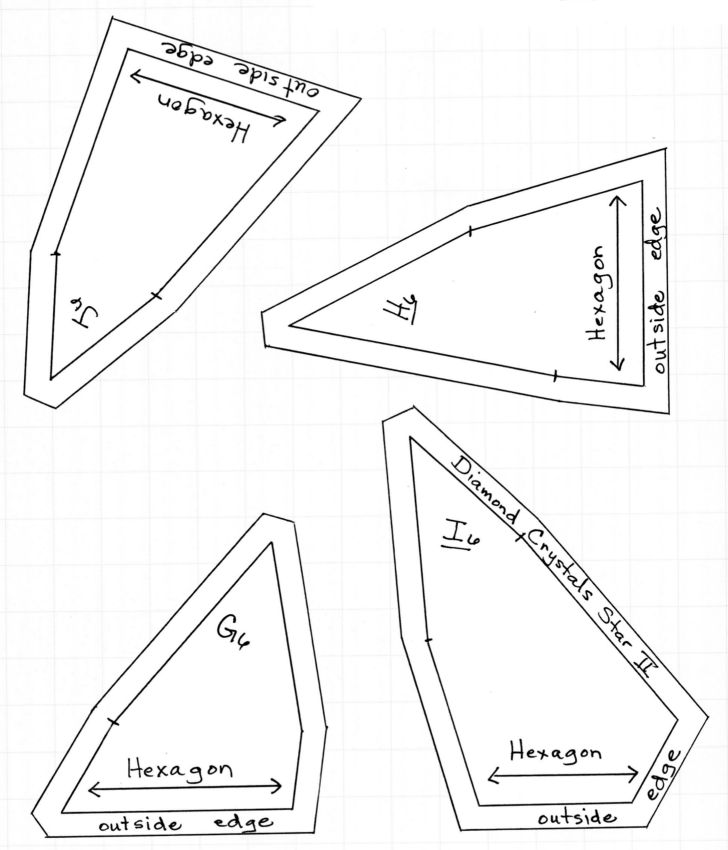

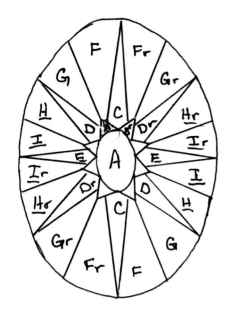

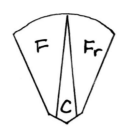

1. Sew F and Fr pieces to corresponding sides of C. Sew both sections.

2. Sew A and Ar to corresponding sides of C at center.

3. Sew I and Ir pieces to corresponding sides of E. Sew both sections.

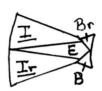

4. Sew Br and B to corresponding sides of E at center.

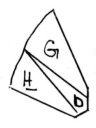

5. Sew G and H pieces to corresponding sides of D. Sew all four sections.

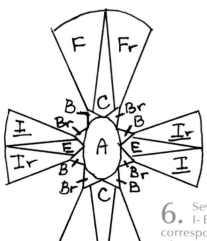

6. Sew F - C - Fr and I- E- Ir sections to corresponding section of center oval.

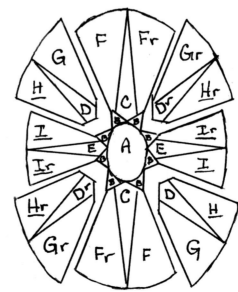

7. Sew sections H- D- G to main compass section with the set-in method, to complete the compass.

49

FABRIC:

1/8 yd- points
1/8 yd- petals
1/2 yd- background

CUT:
(r = reverse)

Solid Points:

C- 2
D- 2
Dr-2
E- 2

Split Points:

Ca-2
Car- 2
Da-4
Dar- 4
Ea- 2
Ear- 2

Backgrounds:

F- 2
Fr- 2
G- 2
Gr- 2
H- 2
Hr-2
I- 2
Ir- 2

Center:

Circle:
A-1

Petals:
B- 4
Br- 4

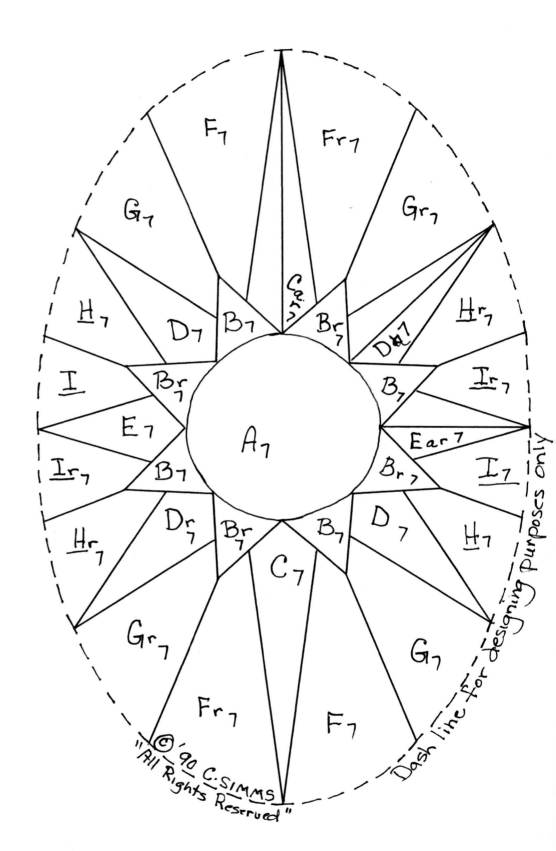

Dash line for designing purposes only

7. OCTAD STAR I
CENTER / SOLID POINTS / SPLIT POINTS

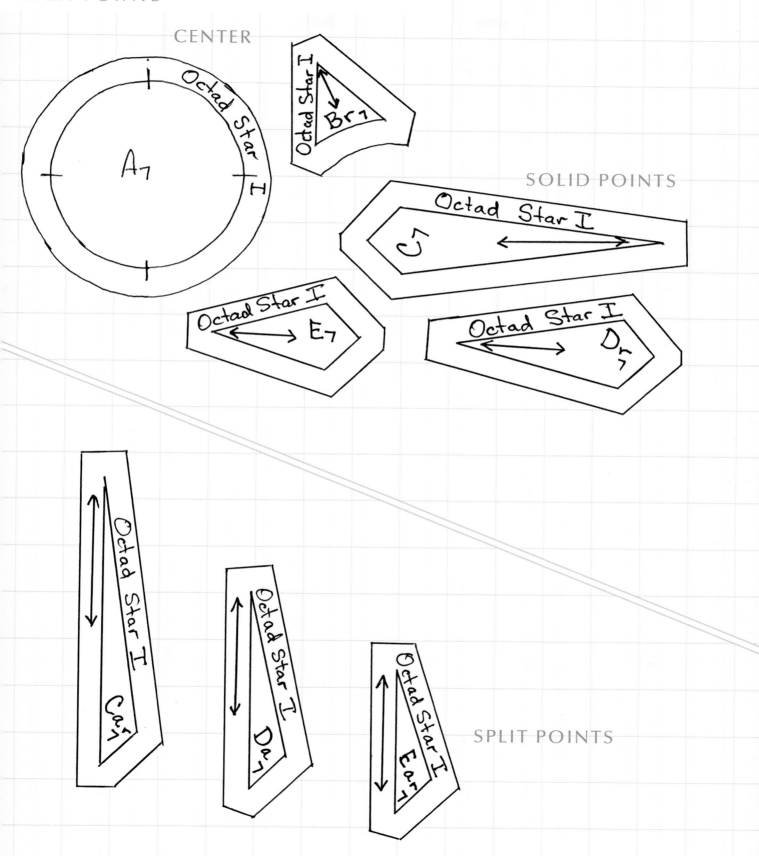

CENTER

Octad Star I

A₇

Octad Star I

B₇

SOLID POINTS

Octad Star I

C₇

Octad Star I

E₇

Octad Star I

D₇

Octad Star I

Ca₇

Octad Star I

Da₇

Octad Star I

Ea₇

SPLIT POINTS

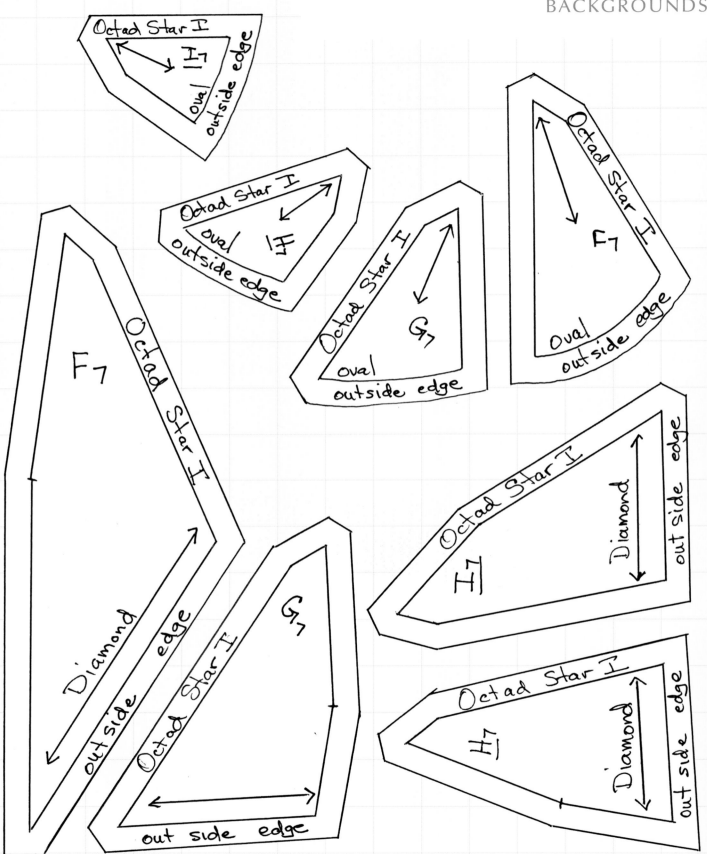

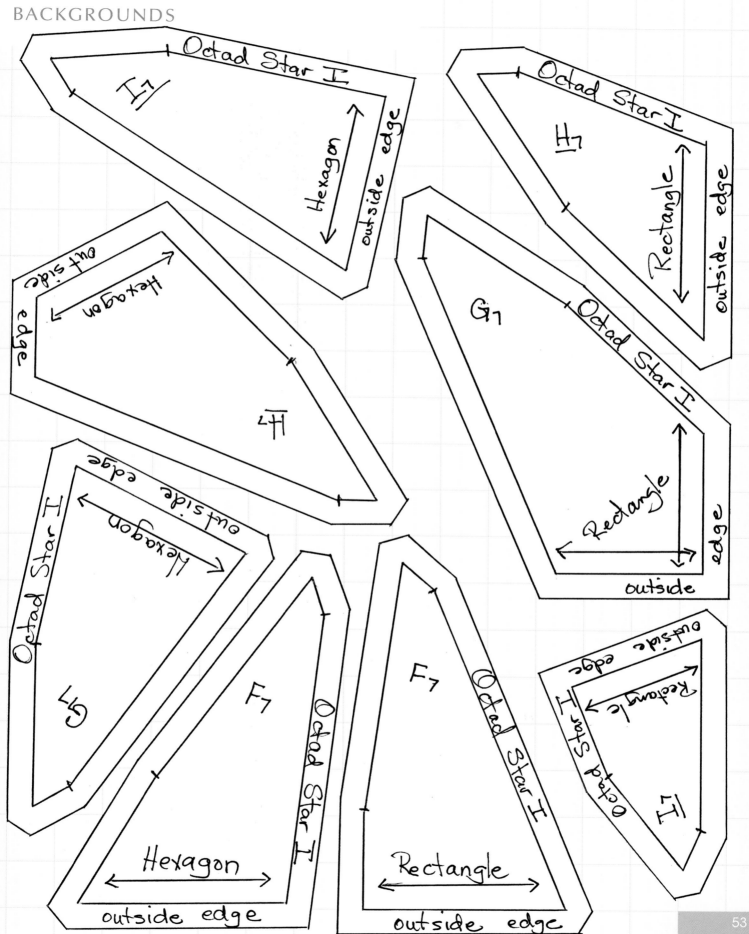

FABRIC:

1/8 yd- petals
1/8 yd- points
3/4 yd- background

CUT:
(r = reverse)

Solid Points:

C- 2
D- 2
Dr- 2
E- 2
Er- 2

Split Points:

Ca- 2
Cb- 2
Da- 4
Db- 4
Ea- 2
Eb- 2

Backgrounds:

F- 2
Fr- 2
G- 2
Gr- 2
H- 2
Hr- 2
I- 2
Ir- 2

Center:

Oval:
A- 1

Petals:
Ba- 2
Bar- 2
Bb- 2
Bbr- 2

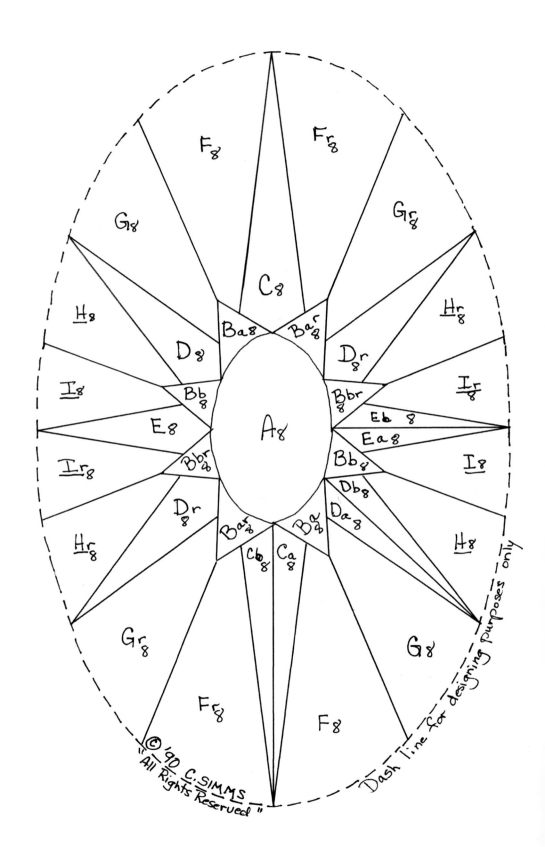

Dash line for designing purposes only

8. OCTAD STAR II
CENTER / SOLID POINTS / SPLIT POINTS

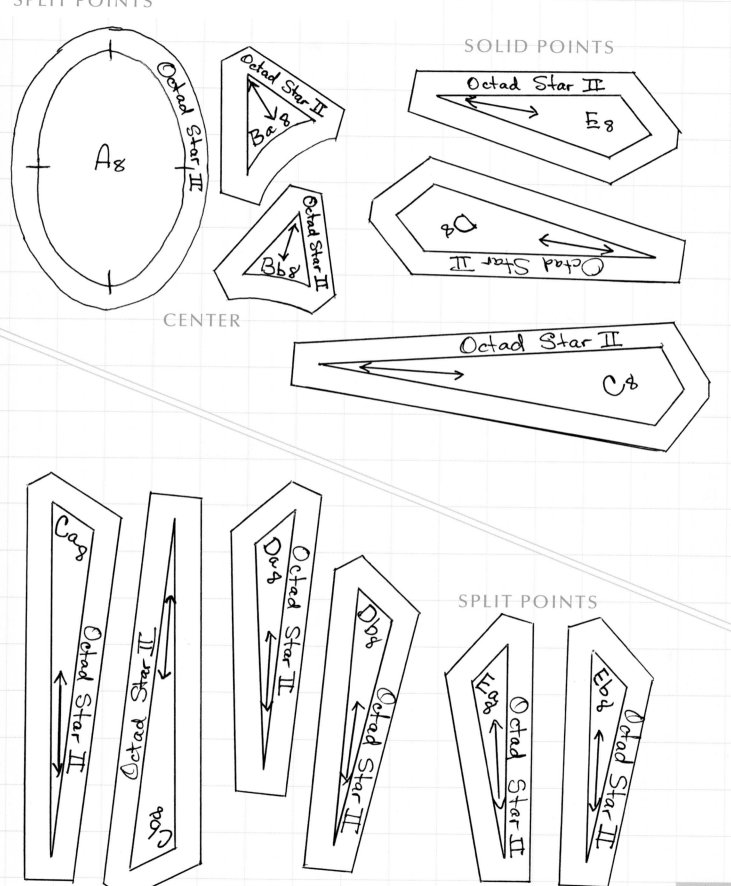

SOLID POINTS

CENTER

SPLIT POINTS

Octad Star II — A8

Octad Star II — B8

Octad Star II — Bb8

Octad Star II — E8

Octad Star II — D8

Octad Star II — C8

Ca8 — Octad Star II

Cb8 — Octad Star II

Da8 — Octad Star II

Db8 — Octad Star II

Ea8 — Octad Star II

Eb8 — Octad Star II

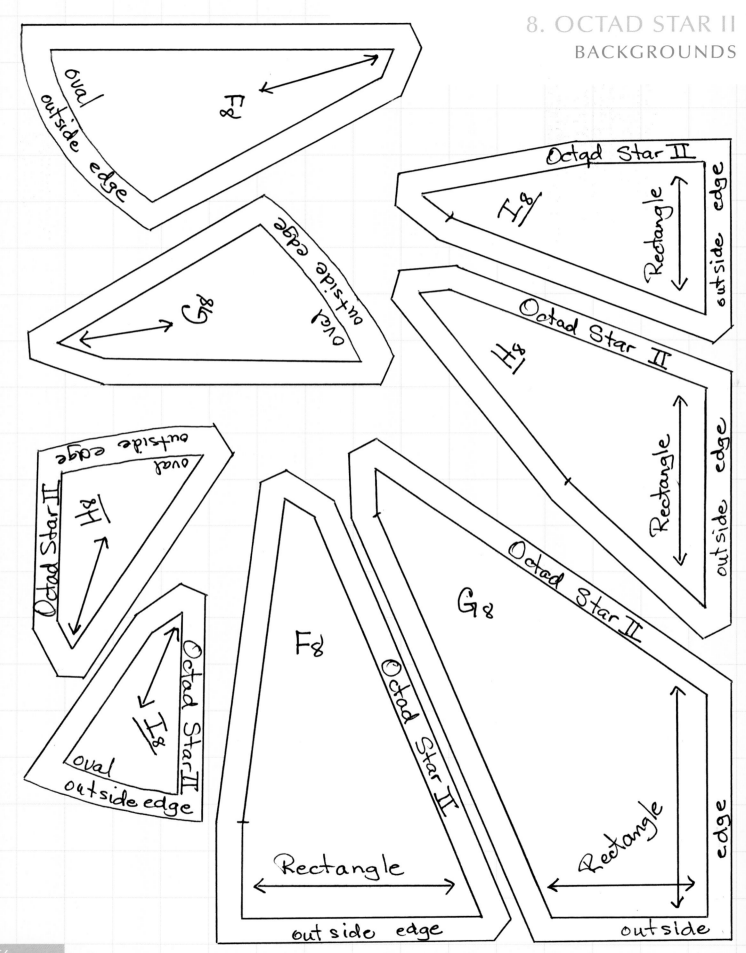

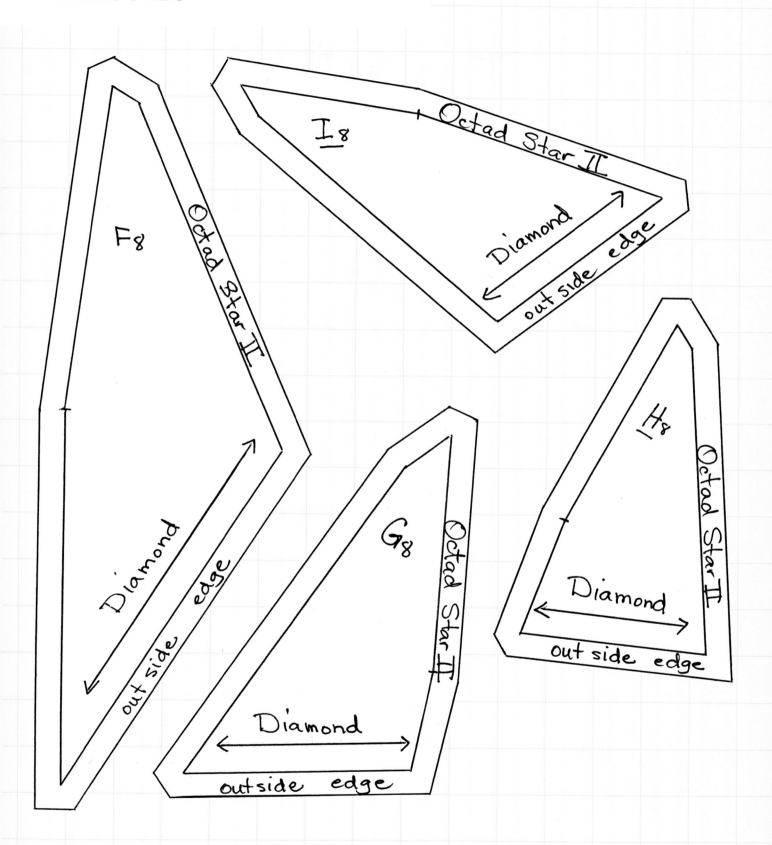

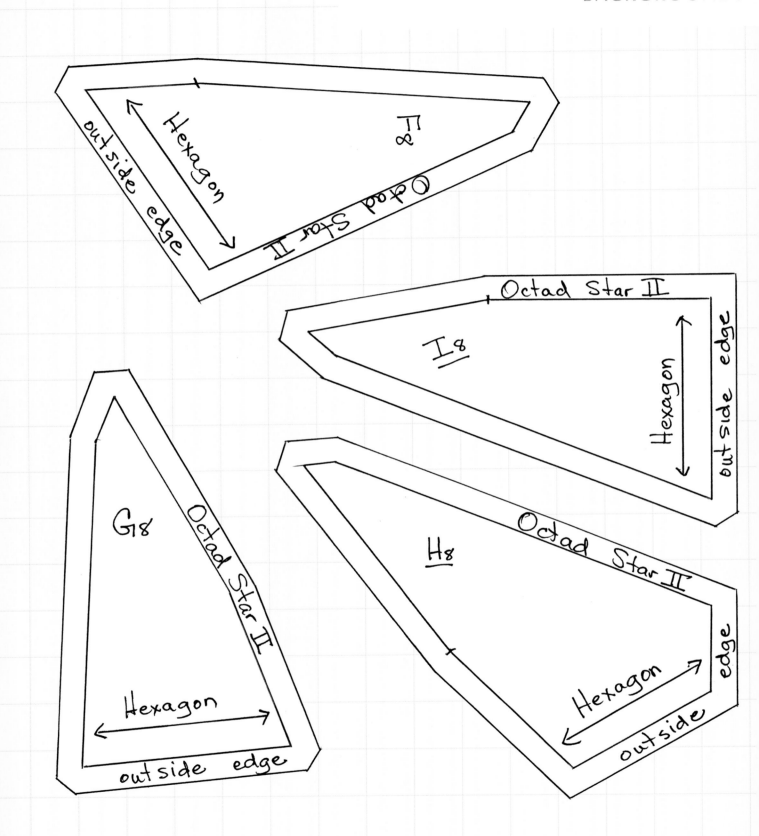

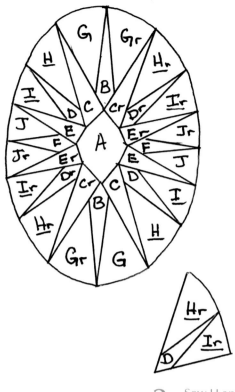

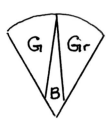

1. Sew G and Gr pieces to corresponding sides of B. Sew both sections.

2. Sew J and Jr pieces to corresponding sides of F. Sew both sections together.

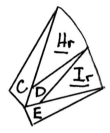

4. Sew C and E pieces to corresponding sides of H-D-I sections. Sew all four sections.

3. Sew H and Ir pieces to corresponding sides of D. Sew all four sections. C

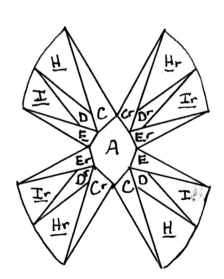

5. Sew C_H_D_I_E sections to corresponding sides of center.

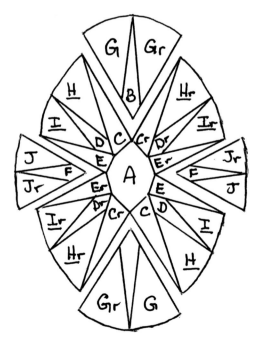

6. Sew sections G-B-G and J-F-J to main compass section with the set-in method to complete compass.

FABRIC:

1/8 yd- 1st row
1/8 yd- 2nd row
1/2 yd- background
center- scrap

CUT:
(r = reverse)

Center:

A- 1 (octagon)

Solid Points:

B- 2
C- 2
D- 2
F- 2

Split Points:

Ba- 2
 Bbr- 2
Ca- 4
 Cb- 4
Da- 4
 Db- 4
Ea- 4
 Eb- 4
Fa- 2
 Fb- 2

Backgrounds:

G- 2
 Gr- 2
H- 2
 Hr- 2
I- 2
 Ir- 2
J- 2
 Jr-2

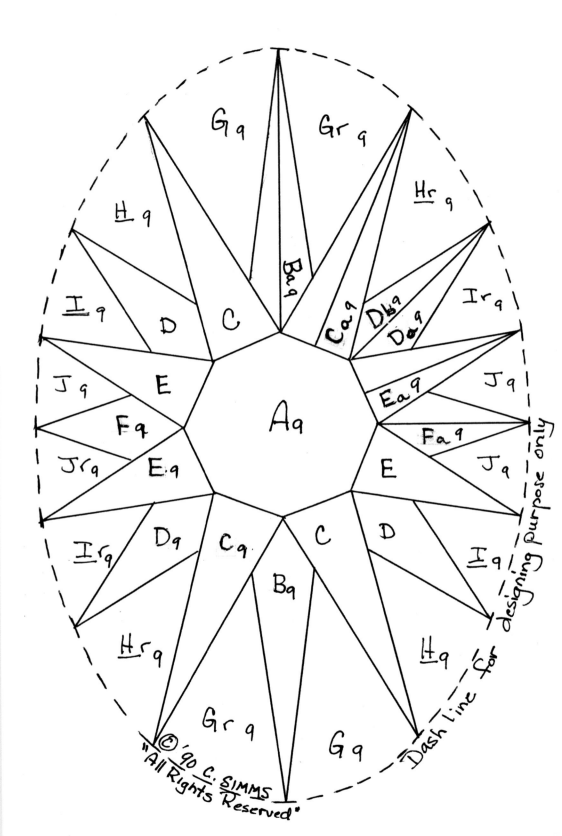

CENTER / SOLID POINTS /
SPLIT POINTS

SOLID POINTS

CENTER

SPLIT POINTS

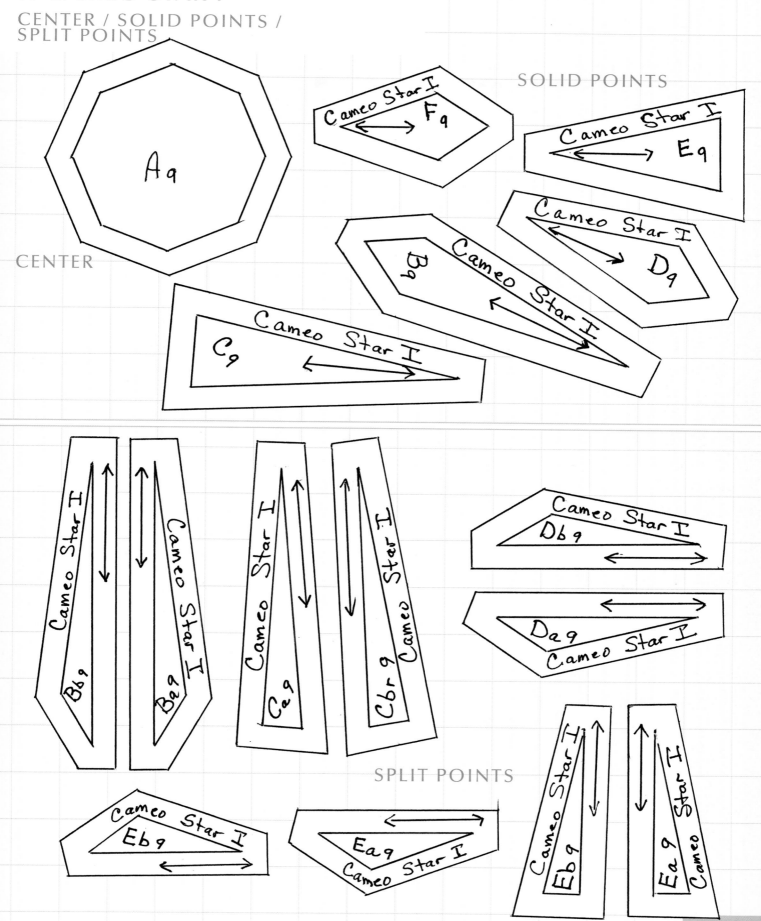

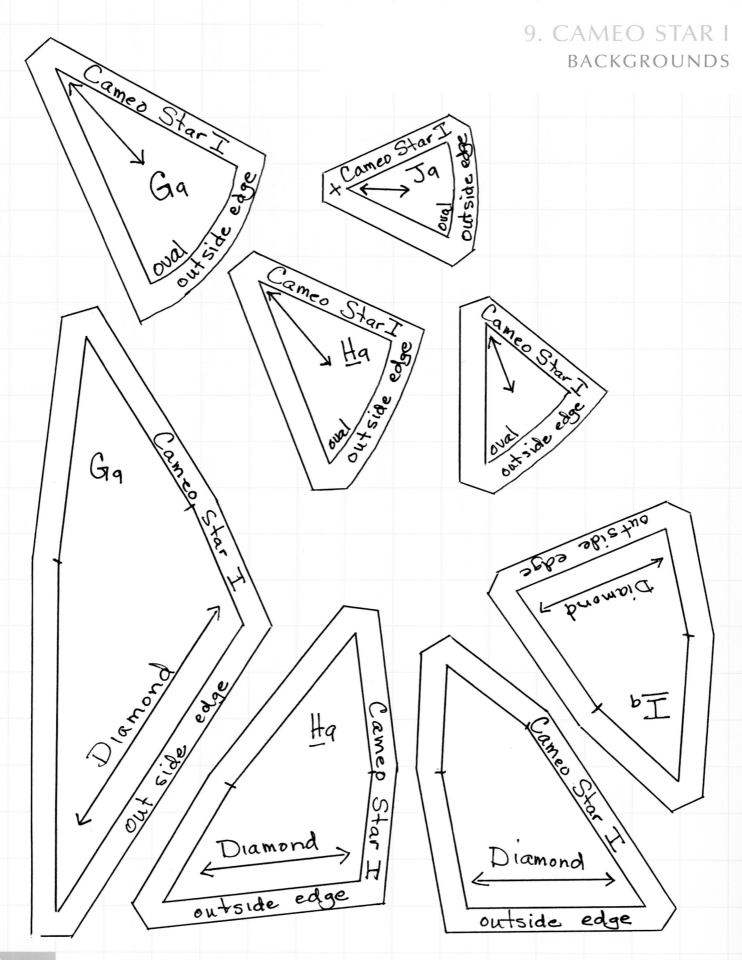

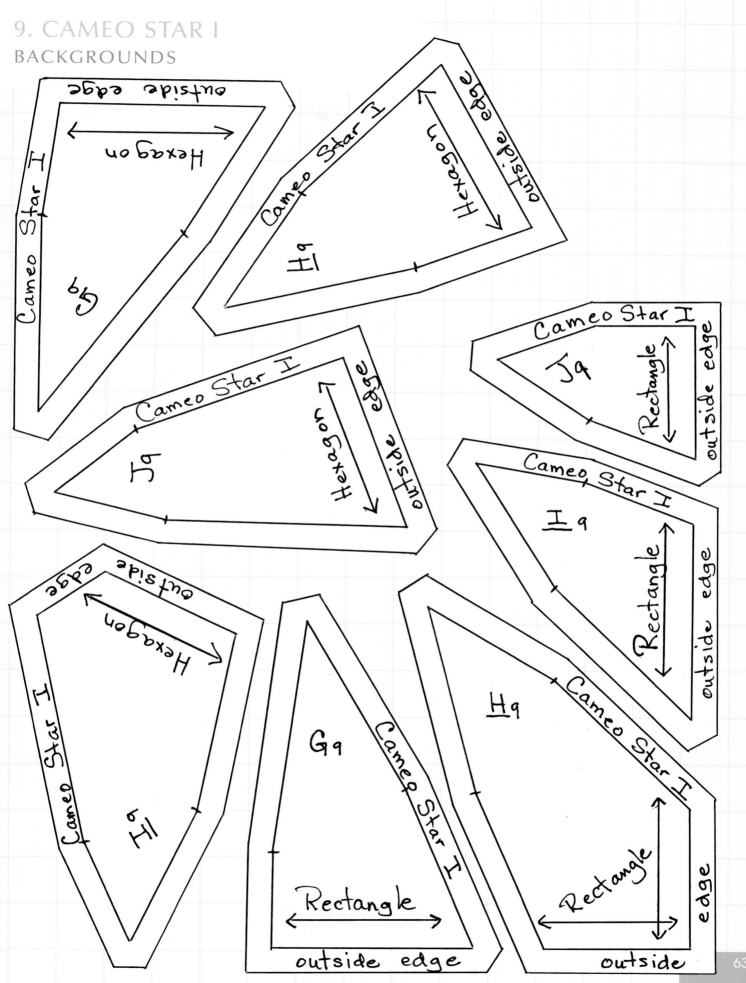

10. CAMEO STAR II
MASTER DRAFT

FABRIC:

1/8 yd- 1st row
1/4 yd- 2nd row
3/4 yd- background

CUT:
(r = reverse)

Center:

A- 1

Solid Points:

B- 2
C- 2
  Cr- 2
D- 2
  Dr- 2
E- 2
  Er- 2
F- 2

Split Points:

Ba- 2
  Bar- 2
Ca- 4
  Cb- 4
Da- 4
  Dar- 4
Ea- 4
  Ear- 4
Fa- 2
  Far- 2

Backgrounds:

G- 2
  Gr- 2
H- 2
  Hr- 2
I- 2
  Ir- 2
J- 2
  Jr- 2

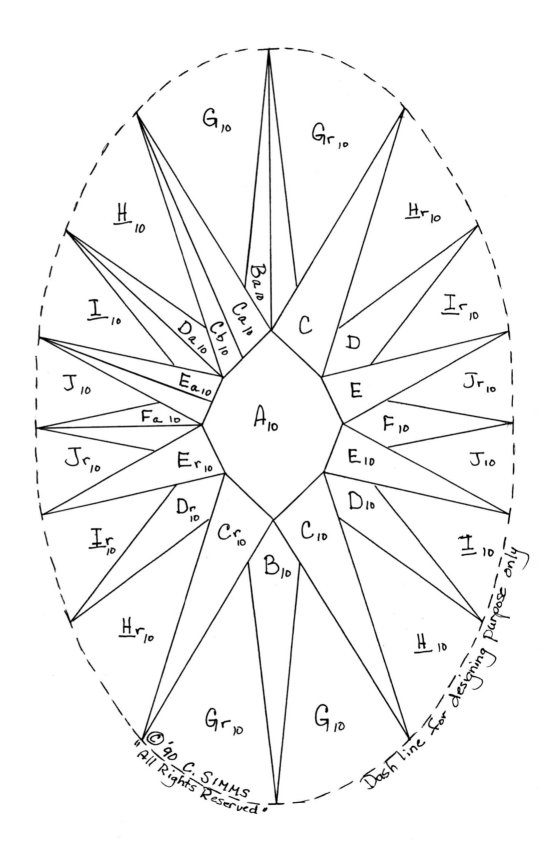

Dash line for designing purpose only

10. CAMEO STAR II
CENTER / SOLID POINTS / SPLIT POINTS

SOLID POINTS

Cameo Star II

A10

CENTER

Cameo Star II

C10

Cameo Star II

D10

Cameo Star II

E10

Cameo Star II

F10

Cameo Star II

B10

SPLIT POINTS

Cameo Star II

Fa10

Cameo Star II

Ea10

Ear Cameo Star II

Cameo Star II

Da10

Cameo Star II

Cb10

Cameo Star II

Ca10

Cameo Star II

Ba10

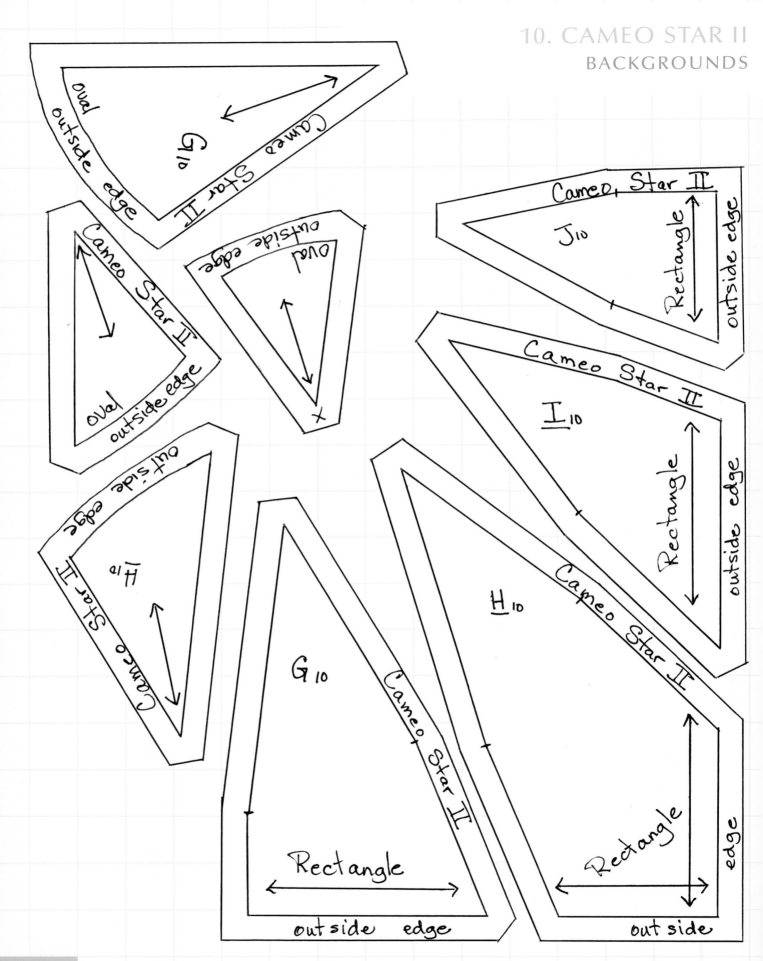

Cameo Star II

G10

oval

outside edge

Cameo Star II

oval

outside edge

oval

outside edge

x

Cameo Star II

H10

outside edge

Cameo Star II

G10

Rectangle

outside edge

Cameo Star II

J10

Rectangle

outside edge

Cameo Star II

I10

Rectangle

outside edge

Cameo Star II

H10

Rectangle

outside edge

Rectangle

edge

out side

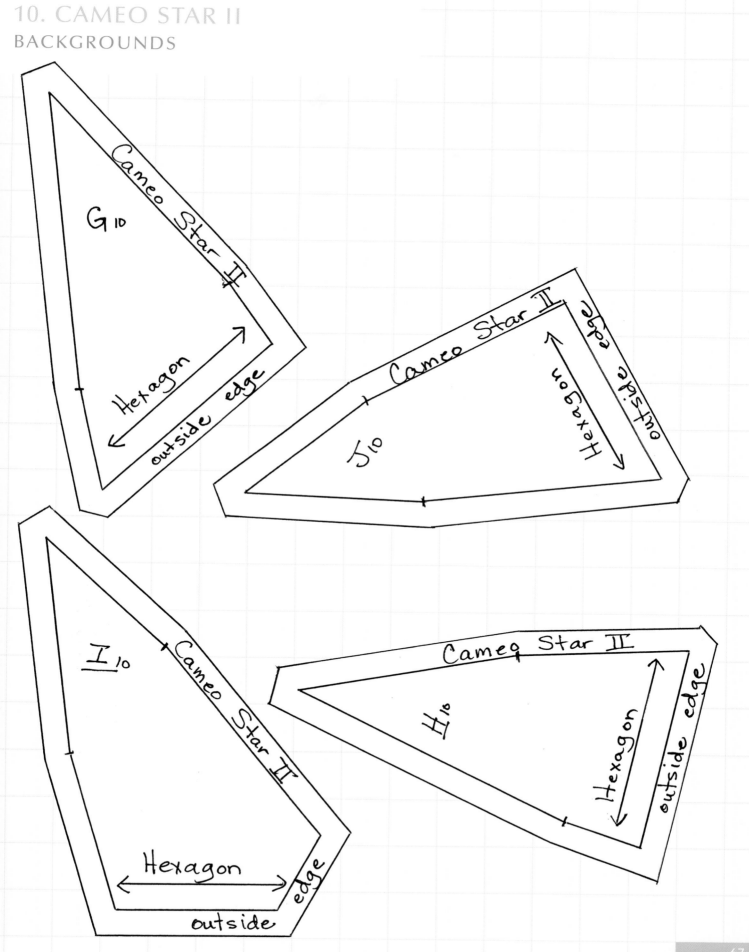

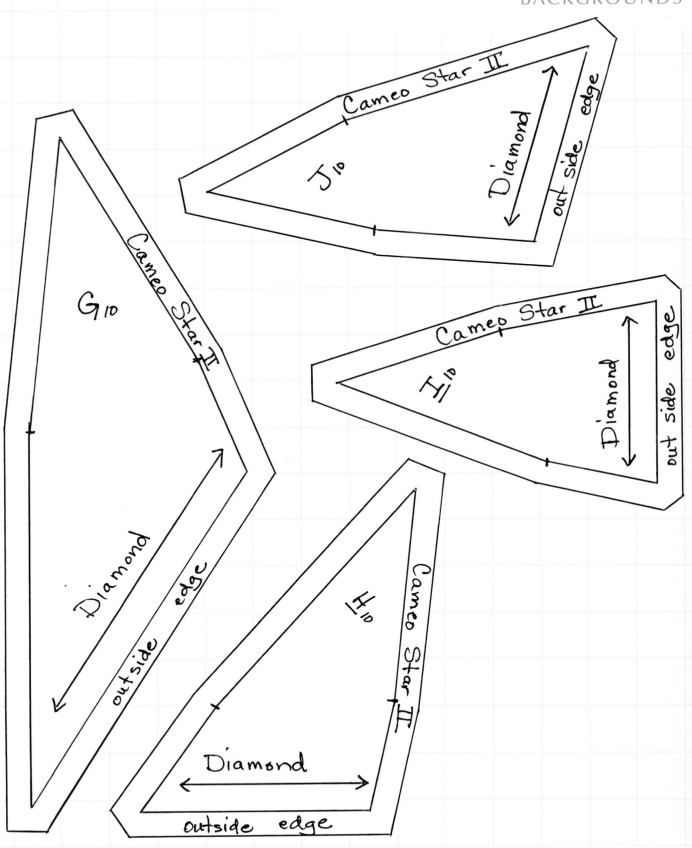

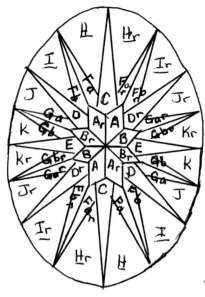

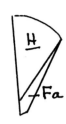

1. Sew Fa pieces to corresponding side of H. Sew all four sections.

2. Sew F-H pieces to corresponding sides of C. Sew both sections.

3. Sew Gb pirces to corresponding side of K. Sew all four sections.

4. Sew Gb-K pieces to corresponding side of E. Sew both sections.

5. Sew A and B pieces to form center star.

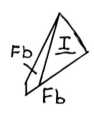

6. Sew Fb pieces to corresponding side of I. Sew all four sections.

7. Sew Ga pieces to corresponding side of J. Sew all four sections.

8. Sew Fb-I and Ga-J pieces sto corresponding sides of D. Sew all four sections.

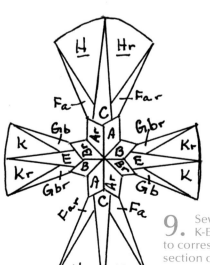

9. Sew H-C-H and K-E-K pieces to corresponding section of star.

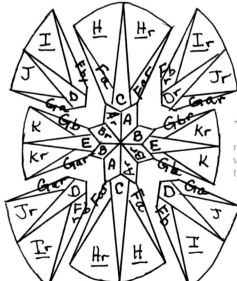

10. Sew I-D-J sections to main compass section with the set-in method to complete compass.

11. MORNING STAR I
MASTER DRAFT

FABRIC:

1/8 yd- star (A/B)
1/8 yd- 1st row
1/8 yd- 2nd row
1/2 yd- background

CUT:
(r = reverse)

Center:

A- 1

Solid Points:

C- 2
D- 4
E- 2

Split Points:

Ca- 2
Car- 2
Da- 4
Dar- 4
E- 2
Er- 2
Fa- 2
Far- 2
Fb- 2
Fbr- 2
Ga- 4
Gar- 4

Backgrounds:

H- 2
Hr-2
I- 2
Ir- 2
J- 2
Jr- 2
K- 2
Kr- 2

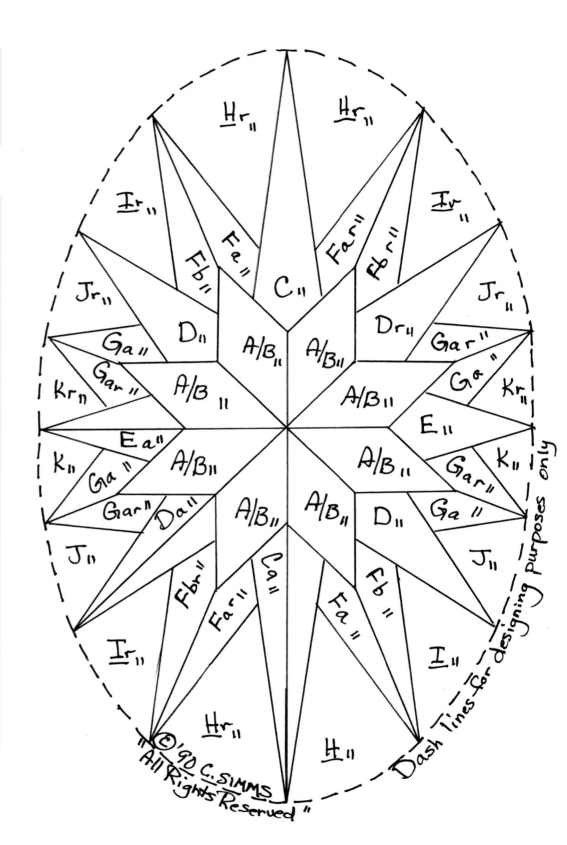

Dash lines-for designing purposes only

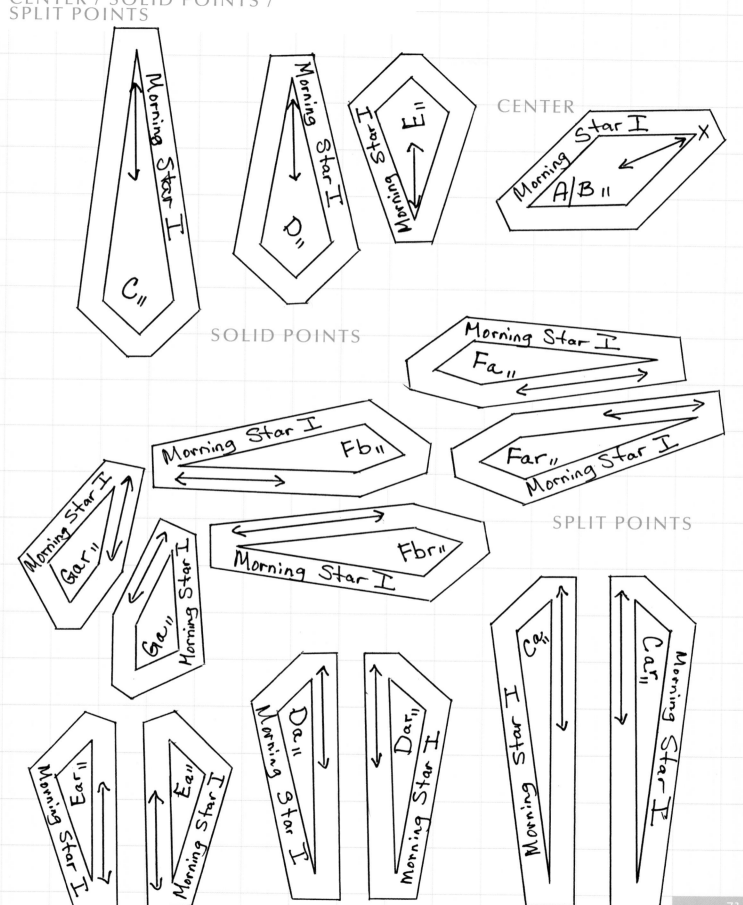

CENTER

SOLID POINTS

SPLIT POINTS

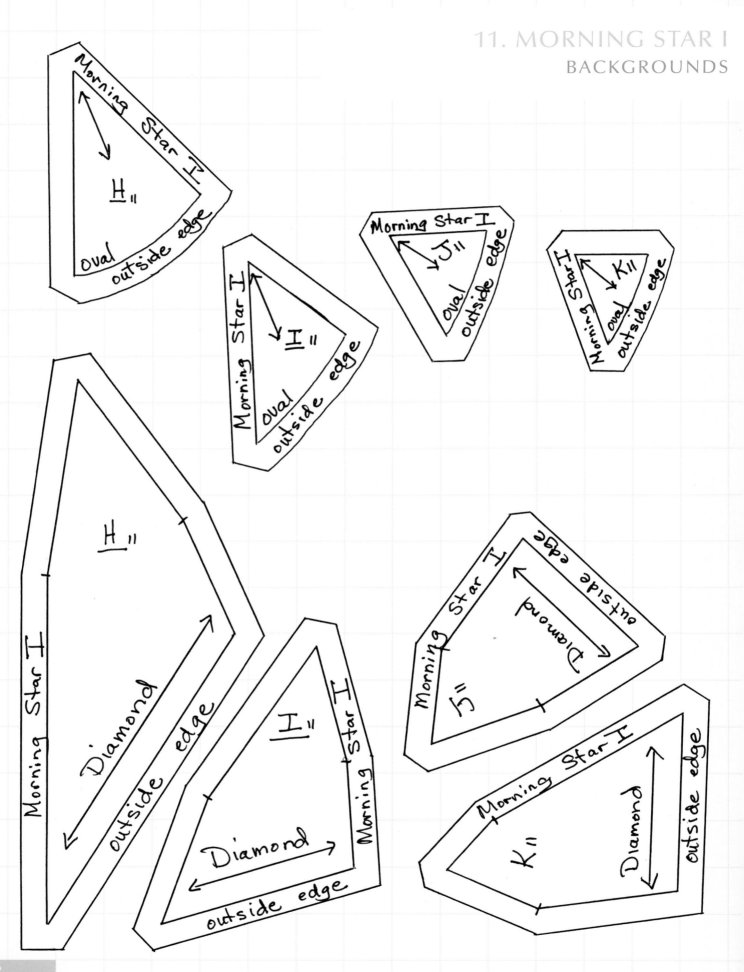

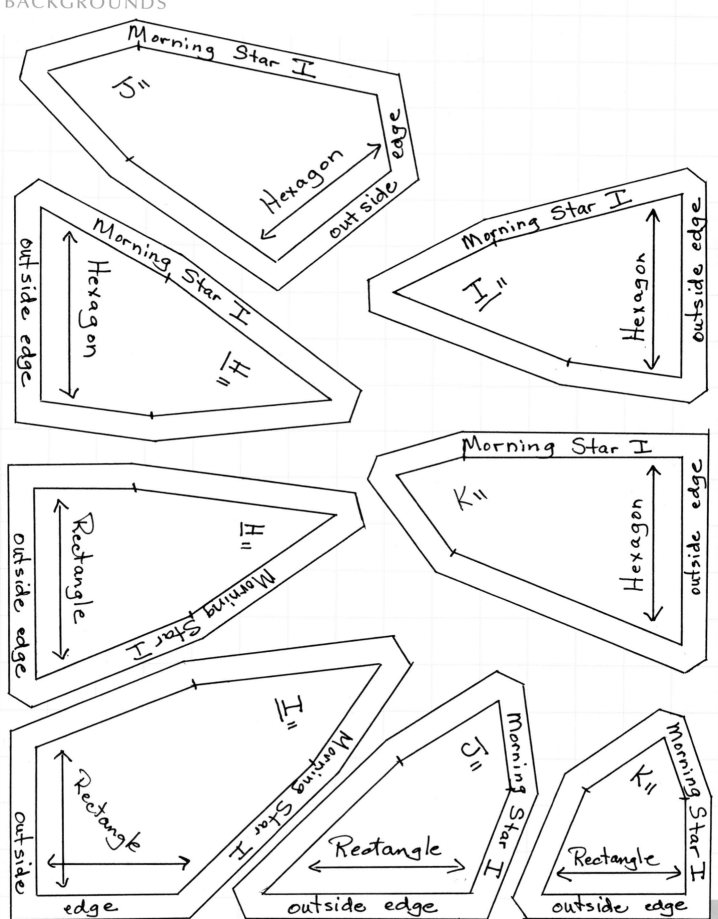

12. MORNING STAR II
MASTER DRAFT

FABRIC:

1/8 yd- 1st row
1/8 yd- 2nd row
3/4 yd- background
scraps- center A/B

CUT:
(r = reverse)

Center:

A- 2
Ar-2
B- 2
Br- 2

Solid Points:

C- 2
D- 4
E- 2

Split Points:

Ca-2
Car- 2
Da- 4
Db- 4
Ea- 2
Ear- 2
Fa- 2
Far- 2
Fb- 2
Fbr- 2
Ga- 2
Gar- 2
Gb- 2
Gbr- 2

Backgrounds:

H- 2
Hr- 2
I- 2
Ir- 2
J- 2
Jr- 2
K- 2
Kr- 2

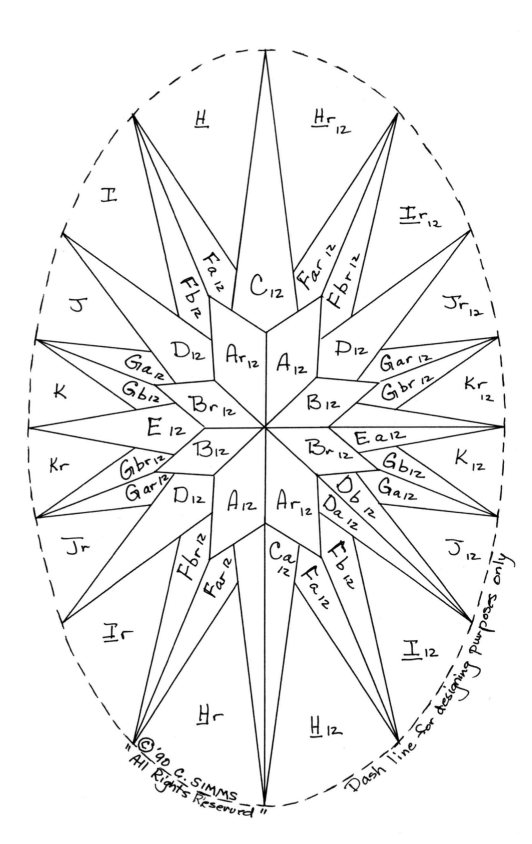

Dash line for designing purposes only

12. MORNING STAR II
CENTER / SOLID POINTS / SPLIT POINTS

Morning Star II — C 12

Morning Star II — D 12

Morning Star II — E 12

Morning Star II — A 12

Morning Star II — B 12

SOLID POINTS

Morning Star II — Fa 12

Morning Star II — Fb 12

Morning Star II — Ga 12

SPLIT POINTS

Morning Star II — Ca 12

Morning Star II — Ca 12

Morning Star II — Da 12

Morning Star II — Db 12

Morning Star II — Ea 12

Morning Star II — Ea 12

Morning Star II — Gb 12

75

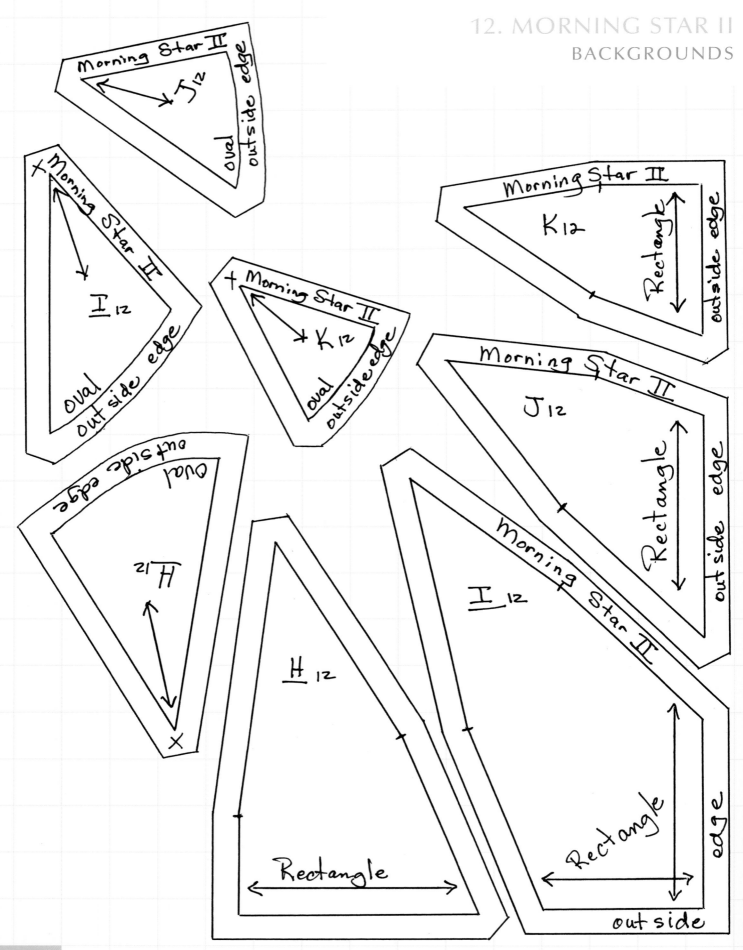

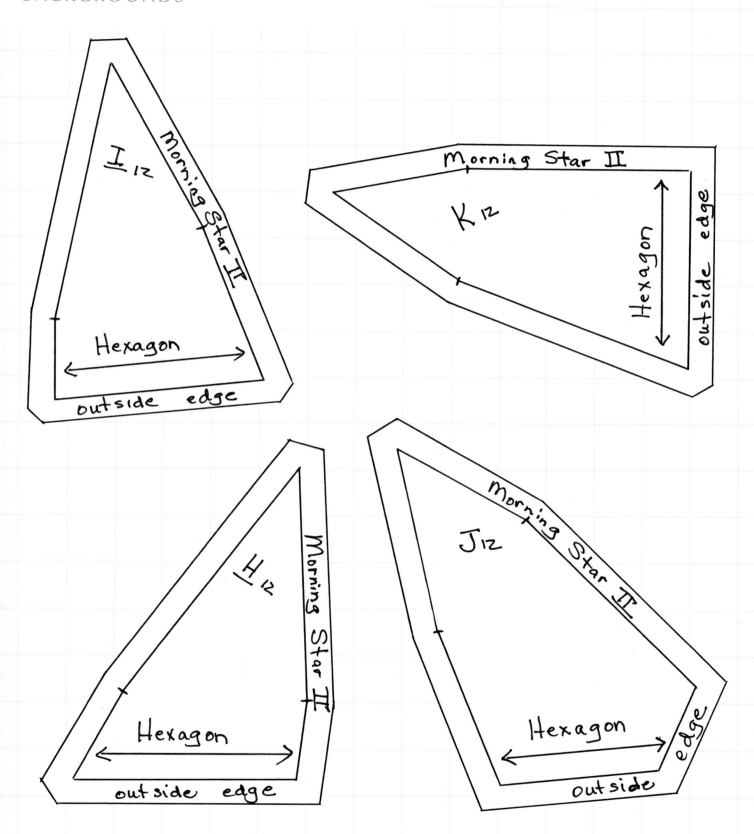

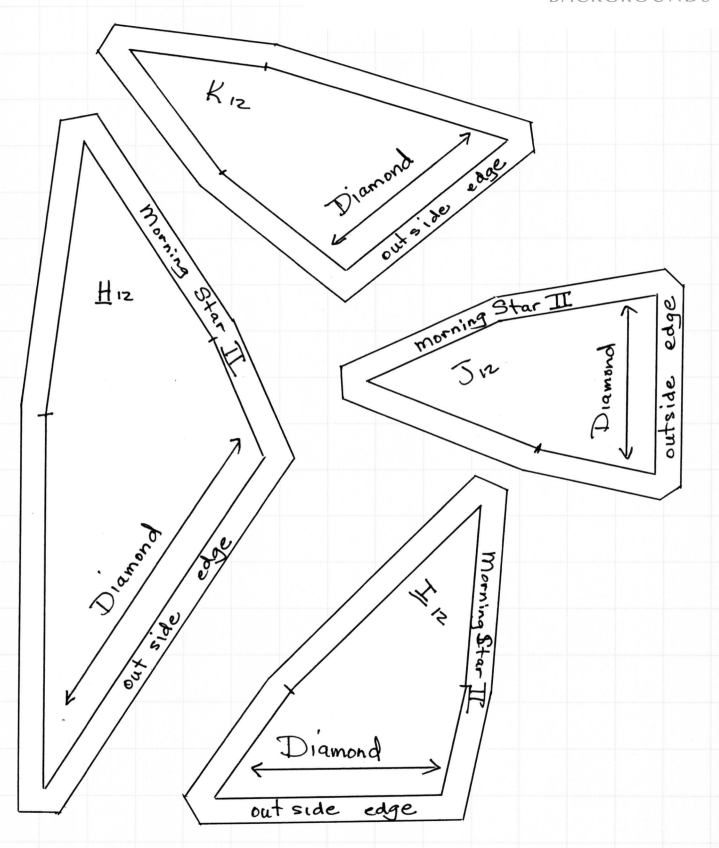

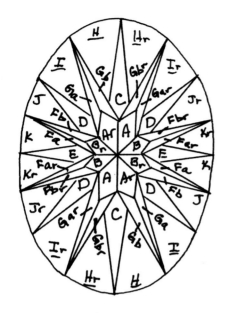

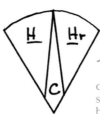

1. Sew H pieces to corresponding sides of C. Sew both sections.

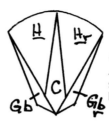

2. Sew Gb pieces to corresponding side of H-C-H. Sew both sections.

3. Sew K pieces to corresponding side of E. Sew both sections.

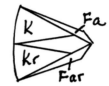

4. Sew Fa pieces to corresponding side of K-E-K. Sew both sections.

5. Sew A and B pieces to form a star.

6. Sew I and J pieces to corresponding sides of D. Sew all four sections.

7. Sew Ga and Fb pieces to corresponding sides of I-D-J. Sew all four sections.

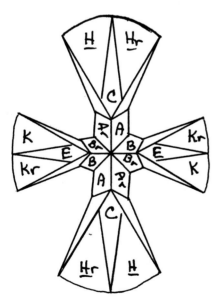

8. Sew H-C-H and K-E-K sections to corresponding sections of star.

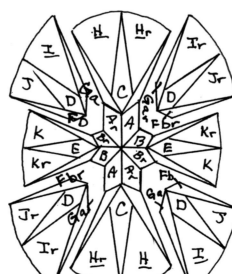

9. Sew I-D-J sections to main compass with the set-in method to complete compass.

13. EVENING STAR I
MASTER DRAFT

FABRIC:

1/4 yd- 1st row
1/4 yd- 2nd row
3/4 yd. background
scraps- star (A/B)

CUT:
(r = reverse)

Center:

A/B- 4
A/Br- 4

Solid Points:

C- 2
D- 2
Dr- 2
E- 2

Split Points:

Ca- 2
Car- 2
Da- 4
Dar- 4
Ea-2
Ear- 2
Fa- 2
Far-2
Fb-2
Fbr-2

Backgrounds:

H- 2
Hr- 2
I- 2
Ir-2
J- 2
Jr- 2
K- 2
Kr- 2

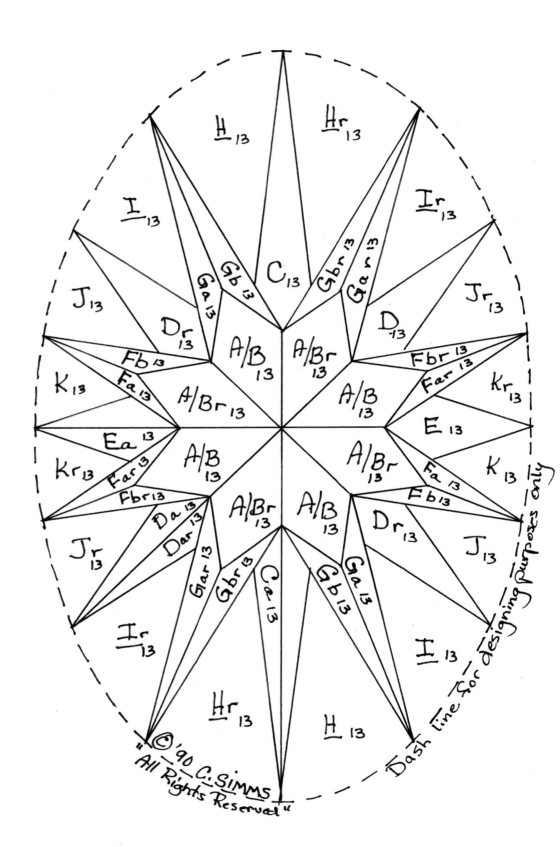

Dash line for designing purposes only

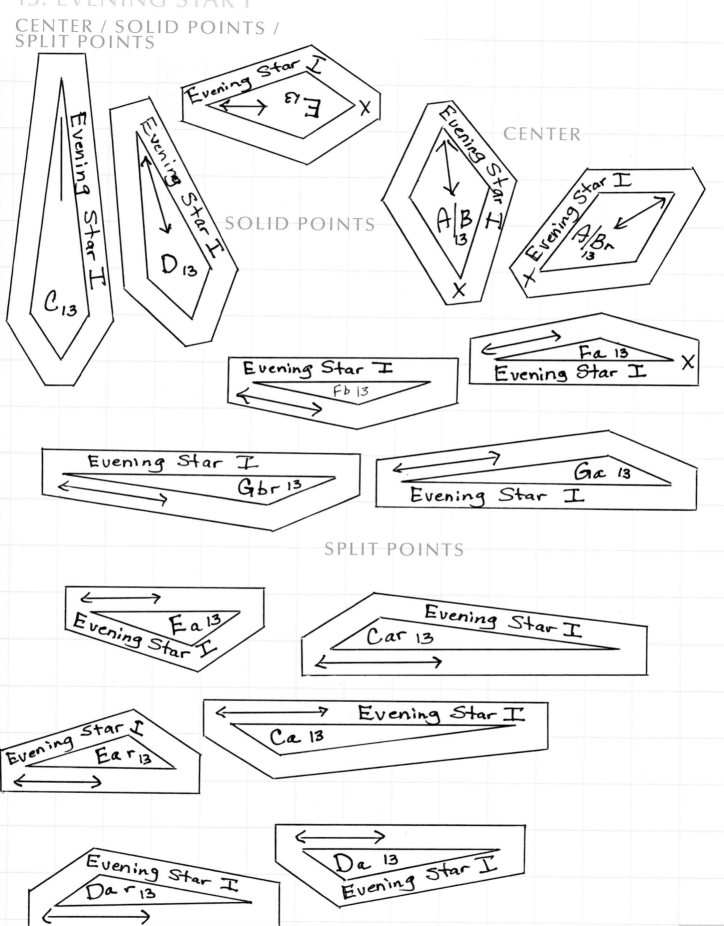

CENTER

SOLID POINTS

SPLIT POINTS

Evening Star I

I 13

Oval

outside edge

Evening Star I

J 13

Oval

outside edge

Evening Star I

H 13

Oval

outside edge

x Evening Star I

K 13

Oval

outside edge

Evening Star I

H 13

Diamond

outside edge

Evening Star I

I 13

Diamond

outside edge

K 13

Diamond

outside edge

J 13

Diamond

outside edge

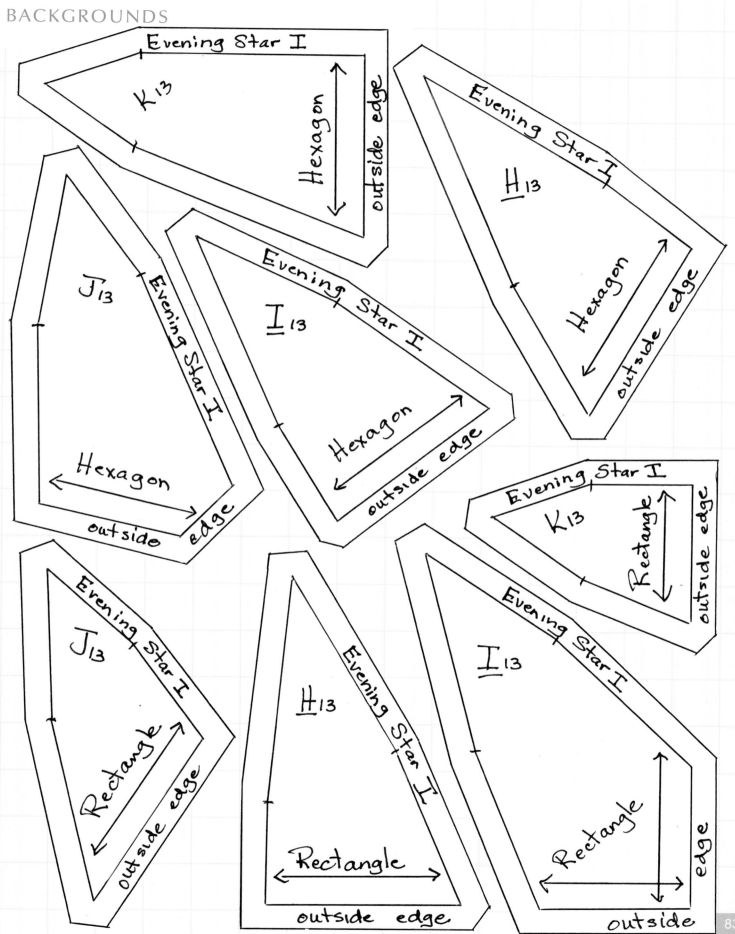

Evening Star I

K 13

Hexagon

outside edge

Evening Star I

H 13

Hexagon

outside edge

J 13

Evening Star I

Hexagon

outside   edge

Evening Star I

I 13

Hexagon

outside edge

Evening Star I

K 13

Rectangle

outside edge

J 13

Evening Star I

Rectangle

outside edge

H 13

Evening Star I

Rectangle

outside   edge

I 13

Evening Star I

Rectangle

outside

14. EVENING STAR II
MASTER DRAFT

FABRIC:

1/8 yd- star (A, B)
1/4 yd- 1st row (F & G)
1/4 yd- 2nd row
  (C, D & E)
3/4 yd- background

CUT:
(r = reverse)

Center:

A- 2
Ar- 2
B- 2
Br- 2

Solid Points:

C- 2
D- 2
Dr- 2
E- 2
Fa-2
Far- 2
Fb- 2
Fbr- 2
Ga- 2
Gar- 2
Gb-2
Gbr-2

Split Points:

Ca- 2	
Car- 2	
Da- 2	Far-2
Dar- 2	Fb-2
Db- 2	Fbr- 2
Dbr- 2	Ga-2
Ea- 2	Gar-2
Ear- 2	Gb-2
Fa- 2	Gbr-2

Backgrounds:

H- 2	J- 2
Hr- 2	Jr- 2
I- 2	K- 2
Ir- 2	Kr- 2

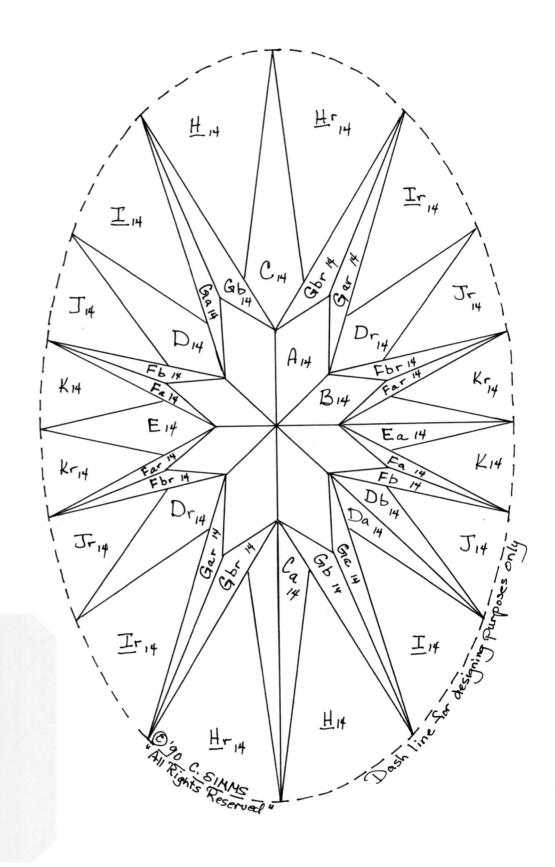

Dash line for designing purposes only

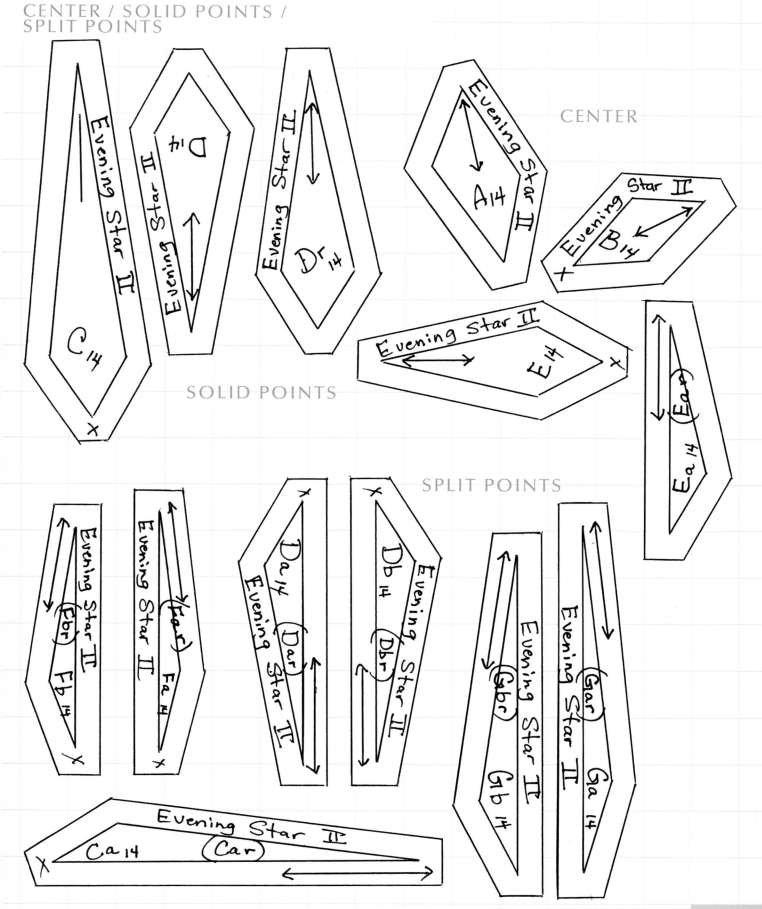

CENTER

SOLID POINTS

SPLIT POINTS

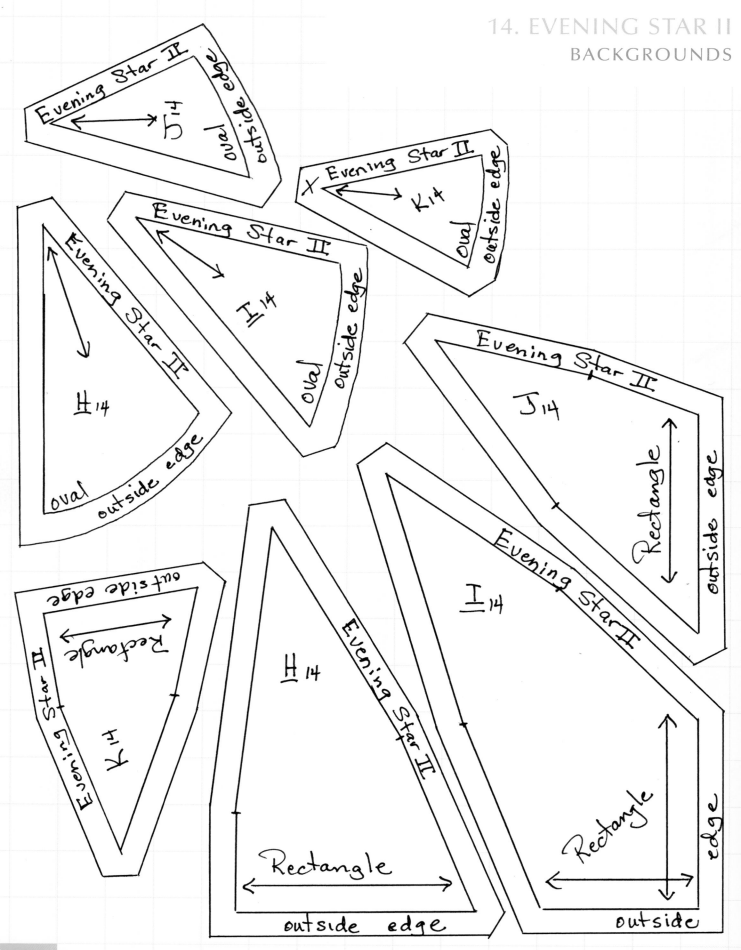

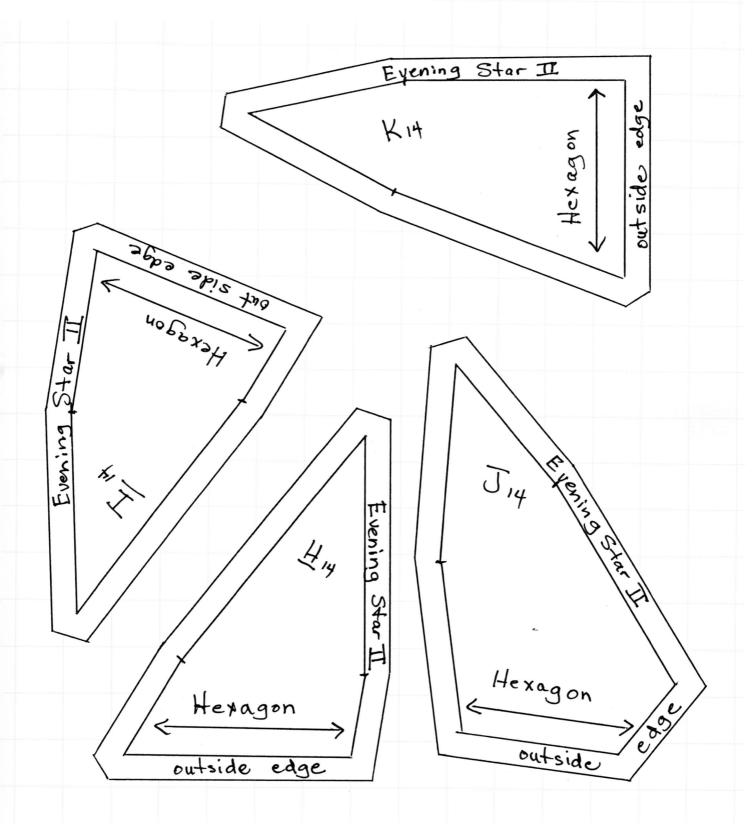

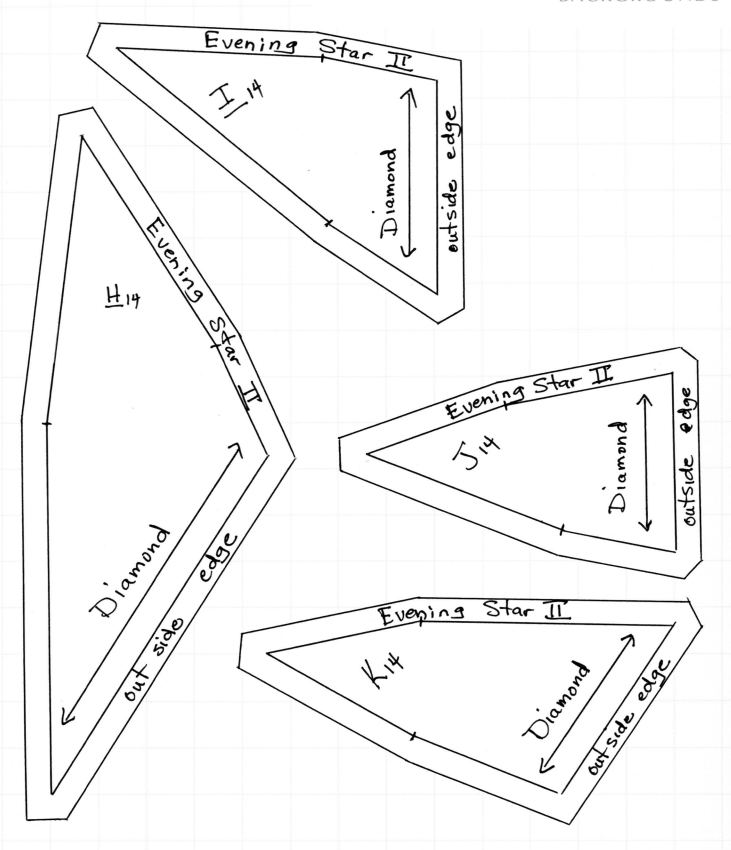

Evening Star II

I 14

Diamond

outside edge

Evening Star II

H 14

Diamond

out side edge

Evening Star II

J 14

Diamond

outside edge

Evening Star II

K 14

Diamond

outside edge

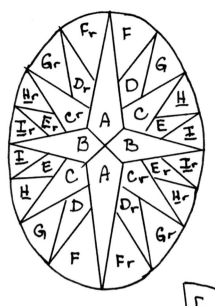

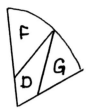

1. Sew F and G pieces to corresponding sides of D. Sew all four sections.

2. Sew H and I pieces to dorresponding sides of E. Sew all four sections.

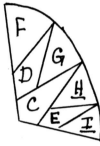

3. Sew F-D-G and H-E-I sections to corresponding sides of C. Sew all four sections.

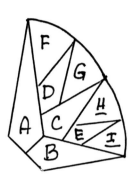

4. Sew A and B pieces sto corresponding sides of 1/4 section of compass. Repeat for opposite 1/4 section.

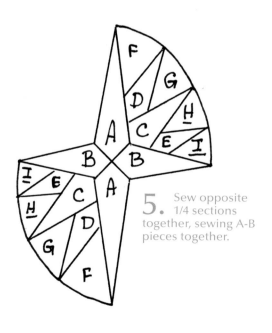

5. Sew opposite 1/4 sections together, sewing A-B pieces together.

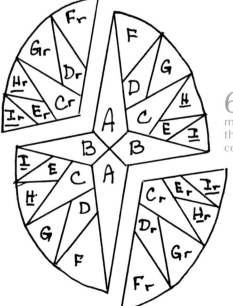

6. Sew in remaining 1.4 sections to main compass, with the set-in method to complete compass.

FABRIC:

1/8 yd- 1st row (A, B)
1/8 yd- 2nd row (C)
1/8 yd- 3rd row (D, E)
1/2 yd- background

CUT:
(r = reverse)

Solid Points:

A- 2
B- 2
C- 2
Cr- 2
D- 2
Dr- 2
E- 2
Er- 2

Split Points:

Aa- 2
Aar- 2
Ba- 2
Bar- 2
Ca- 4
Car- 4
Da- 4
Dar- 4
Ea- 4
Ear- 4

Backgrounds:

F- 2
Fr- 2
G- 2
Gr- 2
H- 2
Hr- 2
I- 2
Ir- 2

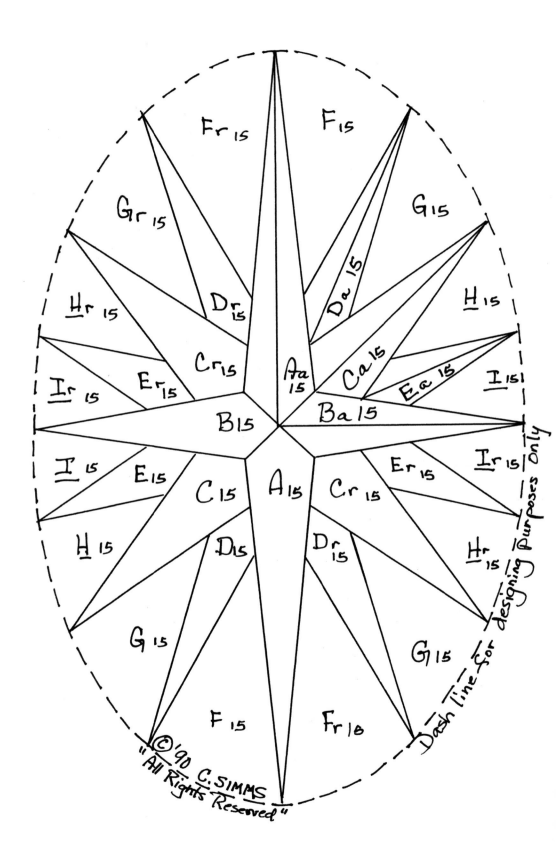

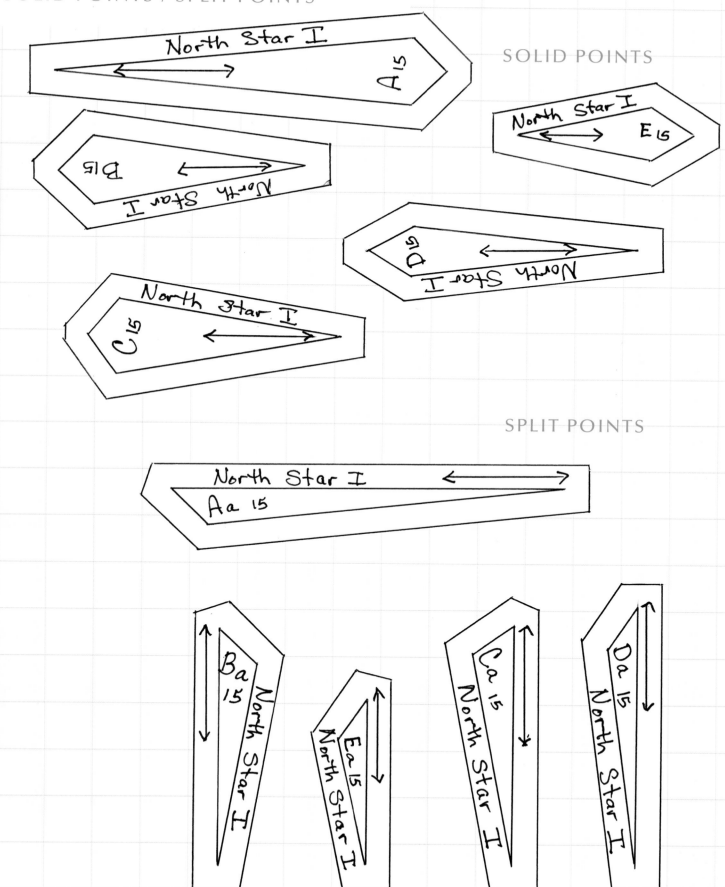

SOLID POINTS

North Star I — A 15

North Star I — D 15

North Star I — E 15

North Star I — D 15

North Star I — C 15

SPLIT POINTS

North Star I — Aa 15

Ba 15 — North Star I

Ea 15 — North Star I

Ca 15 — North Star I

Da 15 — North Star I

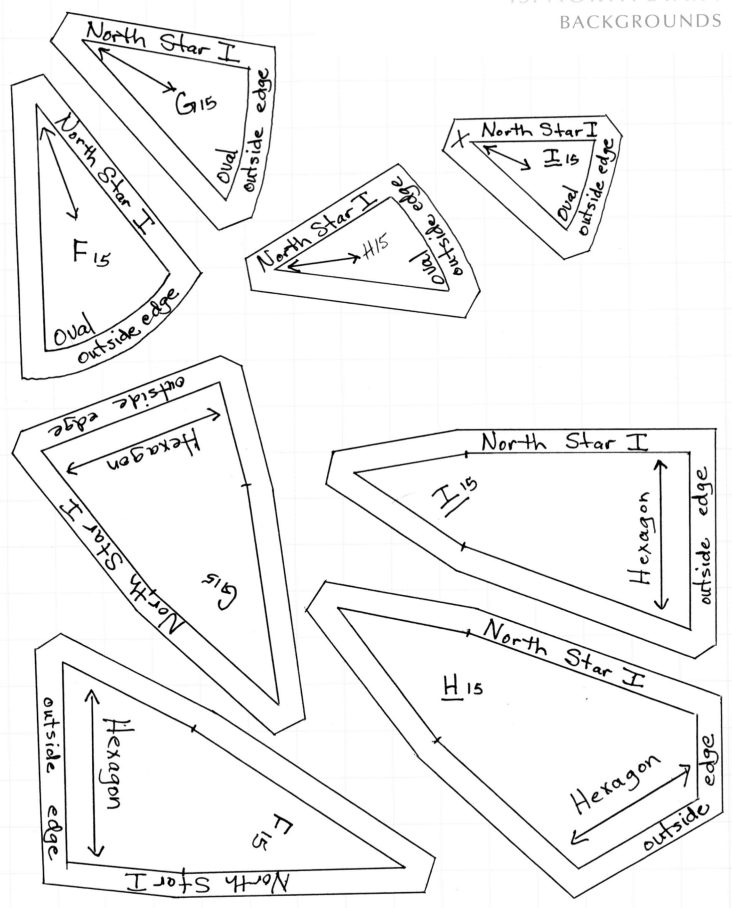

North Star I
G15
Oval outside edge

North Star I
F 15
Oval outside edge

North Star I
H/15
Oval outside edge

X North Star I
I 15
Oval outside edge

North Star I
outside edge
Hexagon
G15

North Star I
Hexagon
outside edge
F 15
North Star I

North Star I
I 15
Hexagon
outside edge

North Star I
H 15
Hexagon
outside edge

92

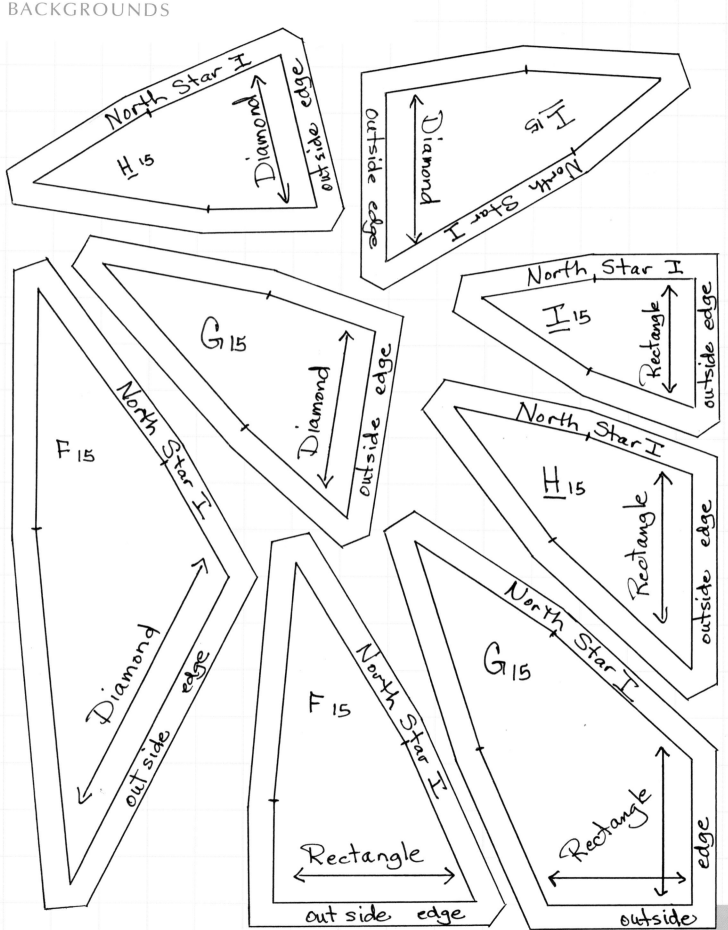

16. NORTH STAR II
MASTER DRAFT

FABRIC:

1/4 yd- 1st row (A, B)
1/4 yd- 2nd row (C)
1/4 yd- 3rd row (D, E)
3/4 yd- background

CUT:
(r = reverse)

Solid Points:

A- 2
B- 2
C- 2
 Cr- 2
D- 2
 Dr- 2
E- 2
 Er- 2

Split Points:

Aa-2
 Aar- 2
Ba-2
 Bar-2
Ca-4
 Car-4
Da-4
 Dar-4
Ea-4
 Ear-4

Backgrounds:

F- 2
 Fr-2
G- 2
 Gr-2
H- 2
 Hr- 2
I- 2
 Ir- 2

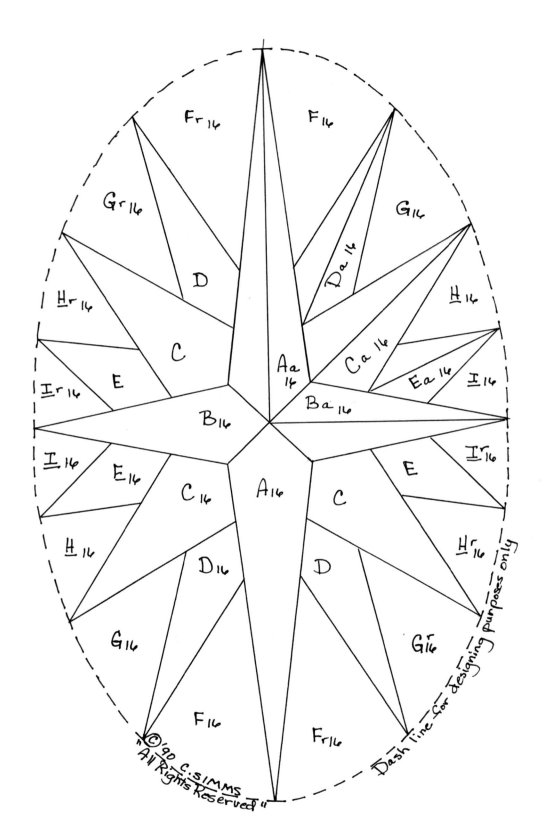

Dash line for designing purposes only

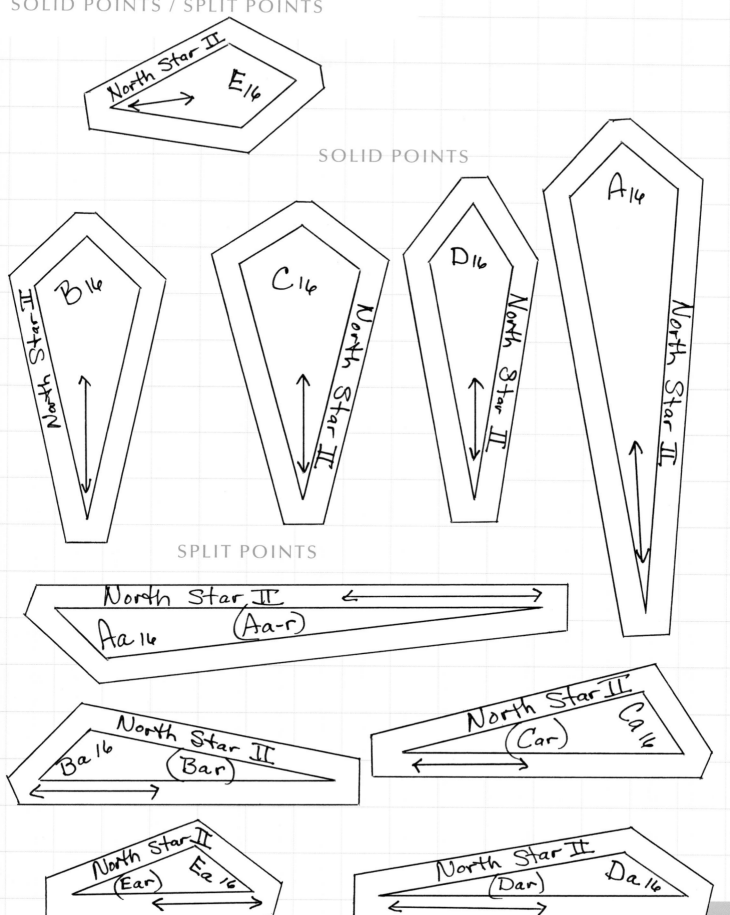

SOLID POINTS

North Star II
E16

B16
North Star II

C16
North Star II

D16
North Star II

A16
North Star II

SPLIT POINTS

North Star II
Aa16   (Aa-r)

North Star II
Ba16   (Bar)

North Star II   Ca16
(Car)

North Star II   Ea16
(Ear)

North Star II   Da16
(Dar)

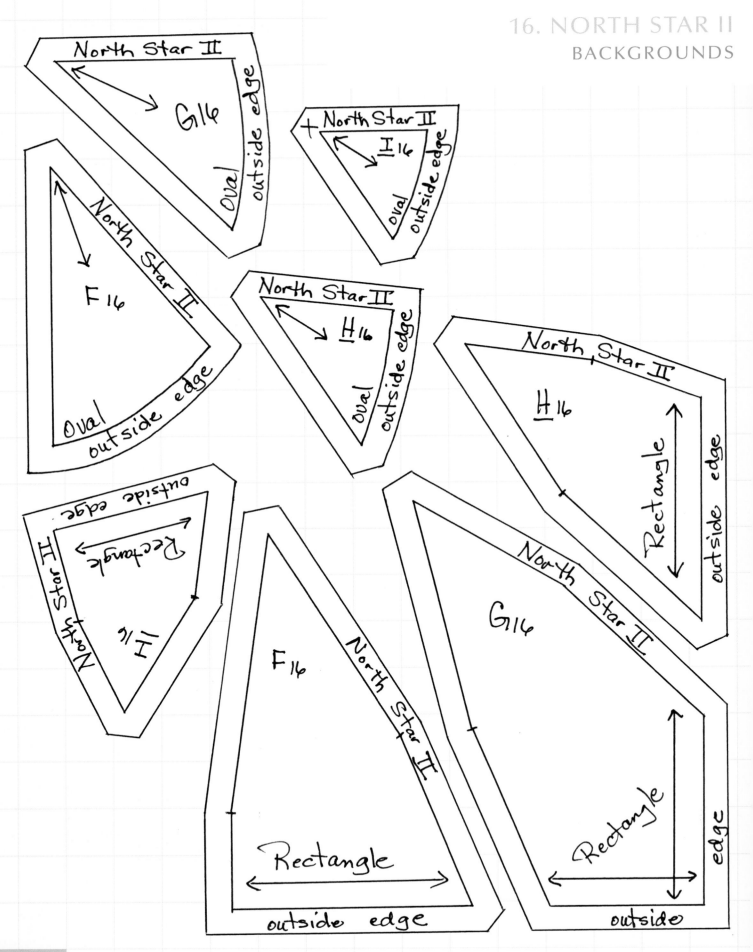

North Star II — G16 — Oval — outside edge

North Star II — I 16 — Oval — outside edge

North Star II — F 16 — Oval — outside edge

North Star II — H 16 — Oval — outside edge

North Star II — H 16 — Rectangle — outside edge

North Star II — H 16 — Rectangle — outside edge

North Star II — G16 — Rectangle — edge

North Star II — F 16 — Rectangle — outside edge

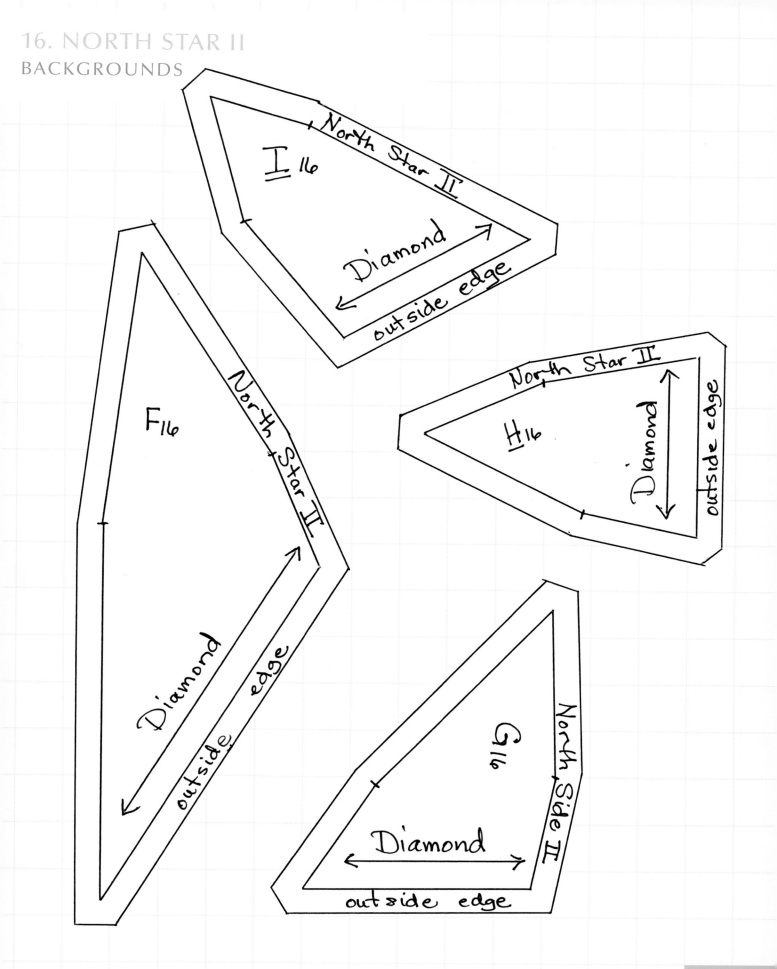

I 16
North Star II
Diamond
outside edge

F 16
North Star II
Diamond
outside edge

North Star II
H 16
Diamond
outside edge

G 16
North Side II
Diamond
outside edge

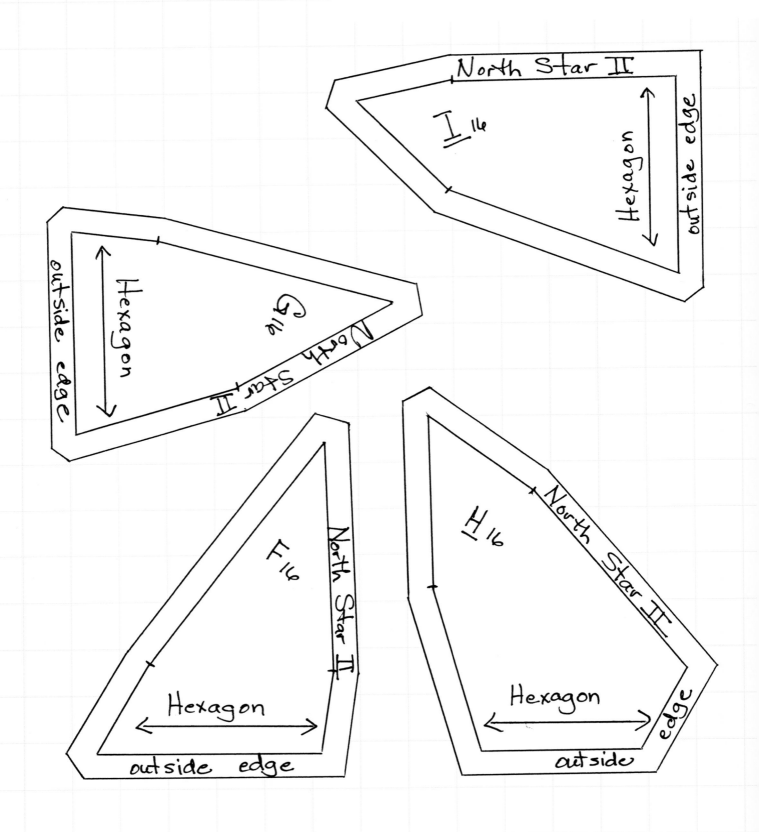

North Star II

I 16

Hexagon

outside edge

Hexagon

outside edge

North Star II

North Star II

F 16

Hexagon

outside edge

H 16

North Star II

Hexagon

outside edge

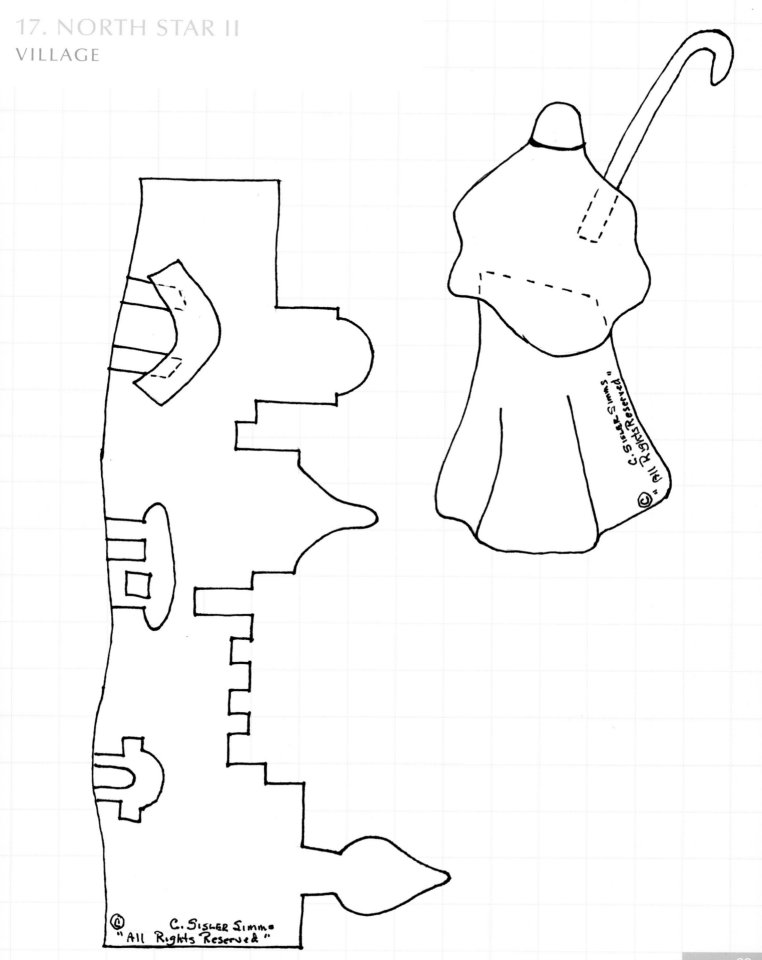

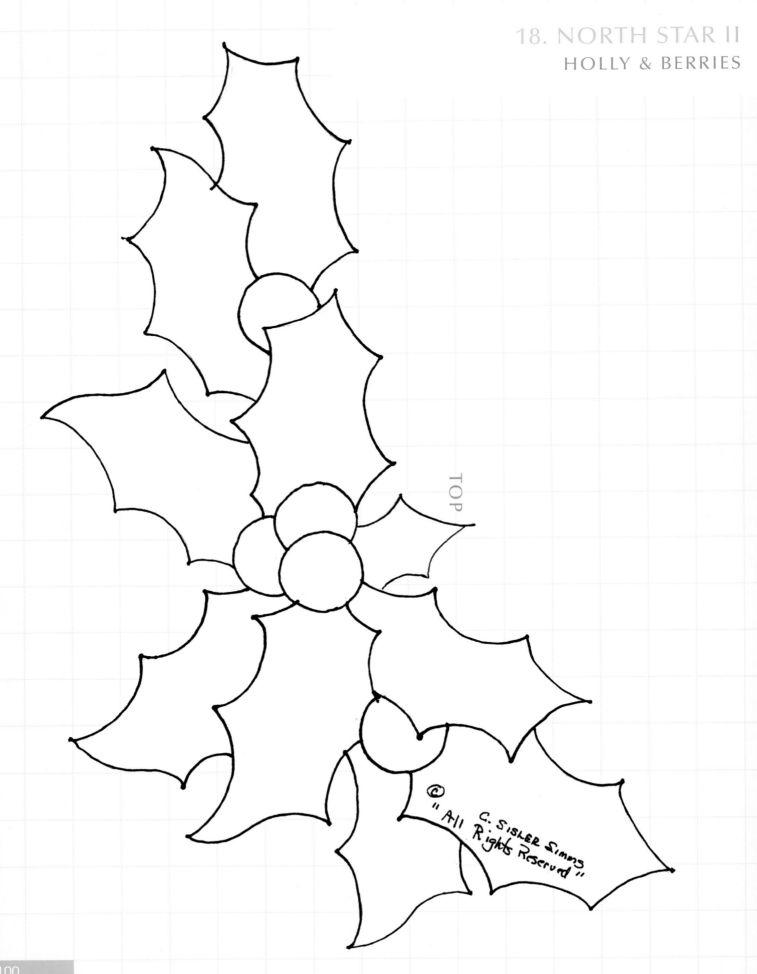

TOP

Outside Background Shapes for Oval Patterns

On the following page, page 102, you will find the rectangle and hexagon outside background shapes, along with both oval shapes. Page 103 contains 1/2 of the diamond shape with the oval seam line.

These outside background shapes are used only if you are making your compass with the curved edge seam.

Decide which outside background shape you are going to use—rectangle, hexagon, or diamond—to correspond to the oval shape.

Enlarge the pattern you choose by 140%. Using freezer paper, trace the outside background shape you are going to use. Add 1/4-inch seam allowances to both the outside edge and the inside curved edge of your chosen shape. These outside background shapes are the only patterns contained in this book to which seam allowances have not been added.

The outside background patterns indicate which size oval shape they correspond with.

If you wish a larger outside background, you may enlarge to your desired size. Do the enlarging before adding your seam allowances.

Now that you have your outside background drafted with seam allowances drawn on freezer paper, you are ready to make your template. Using plastic template material, lay it over the pattern on freezer paper, then trace with a permanent ink pen.

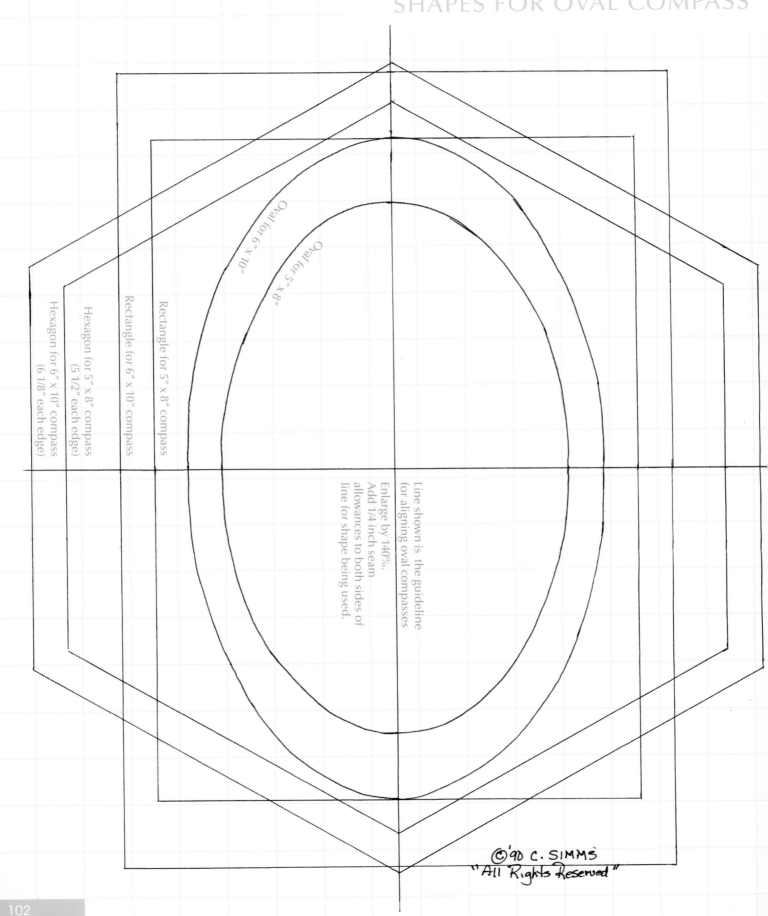

Oval for 6" x 10"

Oval for 5" x 8"

Rectangle for 5" x 8" compass

Rectangle for 6" x 10" compass

Hexagon for 5" x 8" compass (5 1/2" each edge)

Hexagon for 6" x 10" compass (6 1/8" each edge)

Line shown is the guideline for aligning oval compasses
Enlarge by 140%.
Add 1/4 inch seam allowances to both sides of line for shape being used.

© '90 C. SIMMS

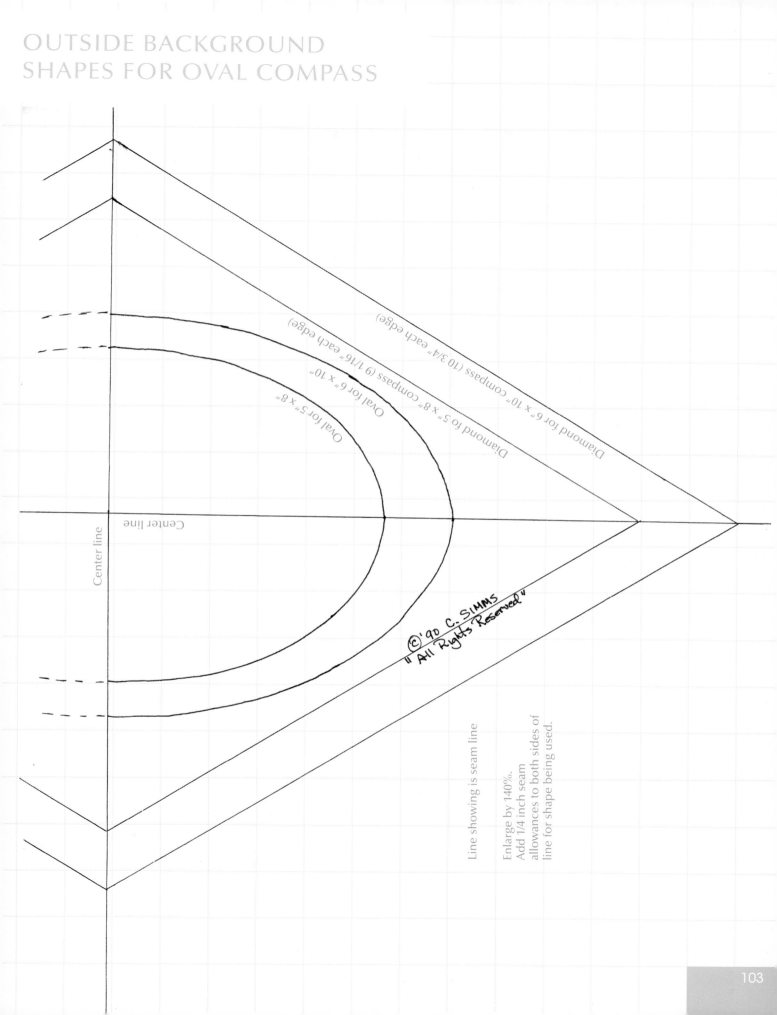

Diamond for 5" x 8" compass (9 1/16" each edge)

Diamond fo 5" x 8" compass (10 3/4" each edge)

Oval for 6" x 10"

Oval for 5" x 8"

Center line

Center line

Line showing is seam line

Enlarge by 140%.
Add 1/4 inch seam
allowances to both sides of
line for shape being used.

Stained Glass
Compass Applique

Some quilters like to do both pieced and appliqued work, but there are others who prefer one or the other. Those of you who don't like to piece patterns but prefer to do applique can still do a Mariner's Compass.

All patterns contained herein can be done in stained glass applique. Use the same patterns with seam allowance as for pieced compass. You will notice that the elongated points have been squared off to eliminate excess fabric. Cut your fabric with the elongated point replaced. (See Fig. 10.1)

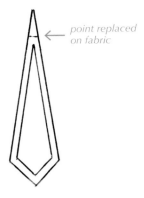

Figure 10.1

From here on, I will refer to the compass as a star. Trace over the star with black ink to darken the lines. Now make a light box. If using window glass, use a thicker piece than ordinary window glass. The same applies for Plexiglas, too. Remember not to lean on either one when using, as both will break. Take the center leaf out of the dining table, and place glass over the opening. If your table doesn't have a leaf you can remove, use two end tables, leaving a space between them to lay glass over. Glass should rest at least two to three inches on both sides of the table or end tables. Now place a small table lamp (without the shade) under the glass.

Lay your star pattern on freezer paper on the glass and tape in place. Determine the placement of the star on the fabric and lay the fabric over the star pattern. Depending on the fabric color, using either white, silver, or lead pencil, trace star points and the center onto the fabric. (See Fig. 10.2)

Figure 10.2

As you cut out your points, you can lay them directly onto the background fabric and either pin in place or use a glue stick.

Your fabric points have seam allowances on them, so that when they are laid out accurately, they should overlap 1/4 inch at appropriate points.

The seam allowances cut edge is a guide line for your 1/4 inch bias tape. Place bias tape along the outside cut edge of points to cover seam allowances and applique down. (See Figs. 10.3 and 10.4)

Applique the outside edge of the bias tape to the outside edge of the point, then go back and sew down bias tape inside edge over the point. Do each point before proceeding to the next.

Starting with points on the bottom or third row, apply bias tape with raw edge of tape under the overlapping point of the second row. Continue until all points are done. The center is done last.

You have the choice of using store-purchased bias tape, or you can make your own. You may use rick-rack in colors or gold and silver metallic.

Use Celtic design techniques to hide all raw edges of bias tape.

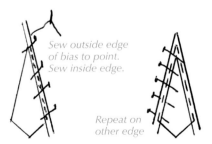

Sew outside edge of bias to point. Sew inside edge.

Repeat on other edge

Figure 10.3   Figure 10.4

Pressing

An important factor in quilting is that seams are never opened up but pressed to one side. This is to give greater strength to a top made up of many different pieces.

For this reason, I feel that pressing is also very important. However, it is very important that you DO NOT PRESS your compass until each block is complete.

A great many individuals use a dry iron to press their squares. I prefer to use the steam setting on my iron for pressing, especially with Mariner's Compasses. As I stated before, 95% of the edges on the compass are on the bias. If your edges have stretched slightly, the steam when pressing will help to shrink them back into place, and this will help your block lay flat.

After each compass block is sewn, press carefully from the back first. This is to ensure that your seams are closed and laying flat. Now, turn over and press the front to block your compass. This front pressing also ensures that your background pieces are not overlapping your points and reinforces the seam pressing.

You may press each compass as soon as it is completed, then lay aside, or you may choose to press after all compasses are completed; however, be sure to press them before they are joined into your top.

When your top is completely joined, press the back and front again. Pressing helps to ensure that the seams do not twist when putting the three layers together.

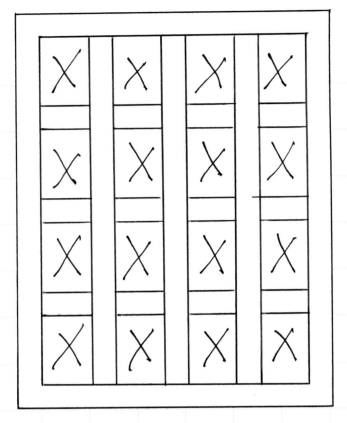

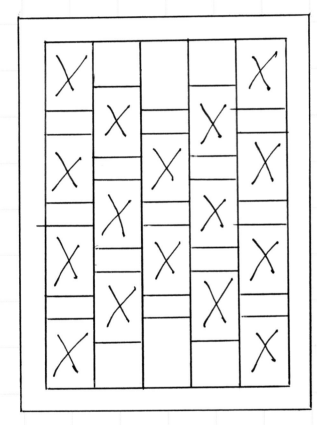

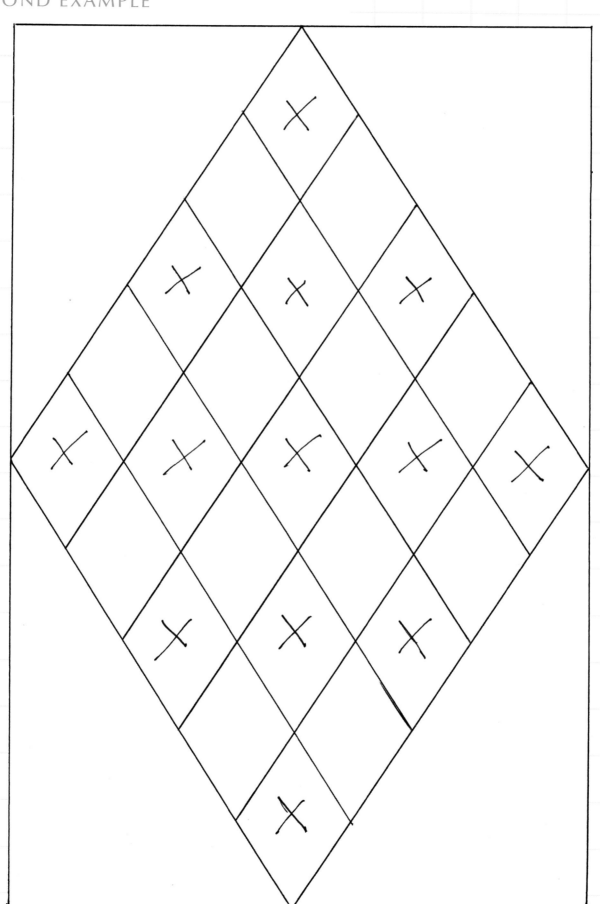

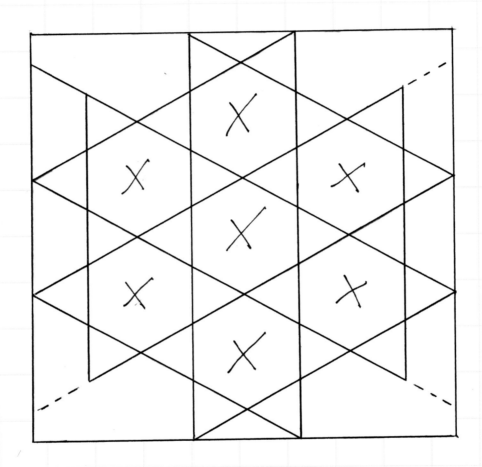

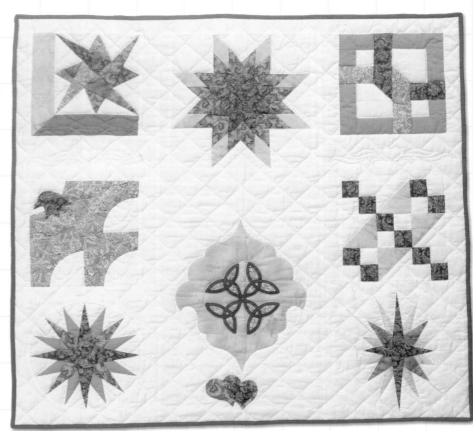

Invitation

Designing these new compasses was fascinating and fun for me. To see them go from paper to fabric was thrilling. But then to have fellow quilters and friends make items pictured within the covers of this book was really exciting. Some had never attempted a compass before, and others have made a round compass. Each have color schemes and ideas that differ from mine.

Even though there are only sixteen compasses here, I have ideas for compasses far different—hopefully for another book!

I hope that these patterns are an inspiration to you to experiment, using your imagination to see what you can achieve in fabric. I would love to see what you accomplish with the ideas and patterns I've shared here. After all, these patterns are for you, designed to spark your creativity

Please send comments, criticism, letters, and photos to me at:

Cynthia Sisler Simms
www.**cindysimms**.net